BEYOND DOGMA

DIALOGUES & DISCOURSES

HIS HOLINESS THE DALAI LAMA

Translated by Alison Anderson

Edited by Marianne Dresser

North Atlantic Books
Berkeley, California

North Atlantic Books
P.O. Box 12327
Berkeley, California 94712

Cover photograph © 1989 Don Farber.
His Holiness the Dalai Lama throwing rice and sending blessings to the crowd below at the Vietnamese Buddhist Temple, Los Angeles, 1989. Photograph by Don Farber for Thubten Dhargye Ling Tibetan Buddhist Center.

Cover and book design by Paula Morrison
Typeset by Catherine Campaigne

Beyond Dogma is sponsored by the Society for the Study of Native Arts and Sciences, a nonprofit educational corporation whose goals are to develop an educational and crosscultural perspective linking various scientific, social, and artistic fields; to nurture a holistic view of the arts, sciences, humanities, and healing; and to publish and distribute literature on the relationship of mind, body, and nature.

Library of Congress Cataloguing-in-Publication Data

Bstan-'dzin-rgya-mtsho, Dalai Lama XIV, 1935–
  [Au-delà des dogmes. English]
  Beyond dogma : discourses and dialogues / Dalai Lama ; foreword by
Steven D. Goodman ; translated by Alison Anderson, edited by Marianne
Dresser.
    p. cm.
  ISBN 1-55643-218-6 (paper)
    1. Buddhism—Doctrines.   I. Anderson, Alison.   II. Dresser,
Marianne.   III. Title.
BQ4165.B7813 1996
294.3'42—fv30
                                                    95-51791
                                                    CIP

1   2   3   4   5   6   7   8   9 / 00   99   98   97   96

CONTENTS

PART IV. BEYOND DOGMA

PART V. INTERDEPENDENCE AND EMPTINESS

FOREWORD
TO THE ORIGINAL EDITION

The purpose of this book is to convey the vision and energy displayed by His Holiness the Dalai Lama during his remarkable visit to France from October 24 to November 16, 1993.

With the exception of the teachings of Buddhist philosophy given at the Institut Vajra Yogini, which were collected and published under the title *Tant que durera l'espace* (Albin Michel, 1994), the text consists of all the public conferences translated from the Tibetan; the presentation has been edited in some cases. The various press conferences and other essentially private meetings which we were fortunate to attend have been arranged by theme and set down in an interview format. We have also included here most of the question-and-answer periods that followed each teaching session at the Institut Vajra Yogini, and in some cases questions taken from the audience at public conferences. We wished to avoid repetition wherever possible and achieve a synthesis that expresses the essential. We apologize in advance for any errors or possible misinterpretations that remain.

Rather than follow the chronological order of events, we have chosen to organize the discourses into five sections. The first presents His Holiness' perspectives on various current social problems. The second deals with the repercussions of the spiritual domain in the political and social world. The third surveys the current situation in Tibet and its future. The fourth, which takes place in the context of an ecumenical meeting in Lourdes, evokes the various opportunities for understanding between religions and addresses individual responsibility, whether or not one is religious. Finally, in conversations between His Holiness and top-level scientists as well as dialogues in response to numerous questions, the fifth section contributes significantly to our understanding of the fundamental principle of interdependence.

We intend this work to be accessible to a large audience. Sanskrit and Tibetan terms retained in the text are noted in parentheses, and are rendered in standard phonetic spellings.

We hope that through these pages the reader will become more aware of the personality and the fundamental message of this remarkable man. The Dalai Lama is extraordinary not only for his humanity but for the utter unpretentiousness with which he assumes the responsibility of being the undisputed spiritual master of Buddhism, which for over 2,500 years has advocated nonviolence, and as the Tibetan head of state confronted with the genocide of its people and the destruction of its environment.

There is a story about the Dalai Lama in Dharamsala, India during an audience with a group of Tibetans who were recent refugees from the "autonomous region of Tibet." As he turned to an old monk sitting beside him, His Holiness suddenly burst out laughing. In 1959, during a stop along the road to exile at a monastery high in the vastness of the Himalayas, this same man had struggled beneath the weight of offerings he was bringing to Gyalwa Rinpoche, the manifestation of Chenrezi, the compassion of all Buddhas, His Holiness the Fourteenth Dalai Lama. We can imagine the old man's emotion—despite the ravages on his face left by more than thirty years of suffering, despite the thousands of people the Dalai Lama has met all over the world since that time, His Holiness recognized him immediately.

It would seem that this is one of the qualities of the Buddha of Compassion—he never forgets anyone he meets. All those who have had the good fortune to come into contact with His Holiness agree that probably the most striking thing about him is the spontaneity and openness with which he approaches others, regardless of their race, gender, age, cultural background, or social position—in short, whoever they might be.

As noted in Buddhist teachings, we must not judge teachers by their charisma, but rather by their words; and we must not put our trust only in the initial meaning of the words alone, but in the deeper meaning they express.

The Translators

May this book contribute to mutual understanding beyond dogma, and thereby to both inner peace and peace on earth.

His Holiness the Dalai Lama
France, 1993

FOREWORD

Tenzin Gyatso, His Holiness the Fourteenth Dalai Lama, is probably the most well known Buddhist on the planet. This "simple Buddhist monk," as he describes himself, has been in the international limelight since the Fifties, when he and thousands of Tibetan men, women, and children fled their homeland into the exiled lands of India and beyond. Recipient of the 1989 Noble Peace Prize, the Dalai Lama is the living embodiment of compassion for tens of thousands throughout Asia, the former Soviet Union, and the West.

Beyond Dogma is a collection of dialogues and discourses culled from His Holiness' 1993 visit to France. Edited so as to preserve the lively, open atmosphere of his meetings with many different groups, the book draws the reader into intimate contact with an astonishing variety of incisive reflections on the problems and possibilities facing humanity as we near the millennium.

The book is organized into five parts. In the first four sections, His Holiness reflects on the myriad social and political problems facing humanity today, and in the last section he responds to questions about the ultimate nature of reality, and our place in the cosmos. While acknowledging the difficult challenges facing all world citizens and their leaders, the Dalai Lama provides hope for the future, based on mindful awareness of opportunities for transformation and preservation of what is most valued and noble. He shows how all dimensions of our interdependent incarnation are involved in this dance of survival and renewal, a dance of the spirit refracted through the prism of habit: psychological, cultural, and political.

In Part One, "Reflections on the Millennium," the Dalai Lama is a savvy political scientist accessing post-Cold War challenges. He begins with a simple observation: Like all people who share this planet, he too is sometimes troubled, confused, and beset with difficulties. As there is no immediate solution to suffering, these problems must be contended with, and therefore it is his habit to emphasize the importance of happiness and satisfaction, which he calls "the very purpose of human existence."

In Part Two, "Spirituality and Politics," the Dalai Lama explores the role of compassion as the foundation for an ethical society. In combination with the cultivation of patience, compassion creates a context for tempering technological education with a moral education. As applied in the international area of human rights, these qualities of compassion and patience can be joined with the active practice of nonviolence founded on kindness and altruism. Such attitudes serve as antidotes to harmful competition, which is the consequence of shortsighted hoarding.

In Part Three, "Nonviolence: An Example to Follow," the Dalai Lama frankly discusses the lessons to be learned from the painful history of Tibet, the future of Tibetan relations with the Chinese government, and the changing role of the Dalai Lama. Always the independent thinker, he mentions the future possibility of a woman Dalai Lama, stating simply "there are no theoretical obstacles." Concerning the desire to engage in armed struggle for a politically independent Tibet, as expressed by many young Tibetans, the Dalai Lama acknowledges their very human frustration while cautioning against giving in to an attitude of violence. This section concludes with "Words of Truth," a poem composed by His Holiness as a prayer for ending the suffering and anguish of Tibet.

In Part Four, "Beyond Dogma," the Dalai Lama sketches out an approach to what might be termed "inner ecumenism," and suggests ways for guarding against seduction by the rigidities of institutional religion, which is often the breeding ground of intolerance. While stressing the importance of harmony between all religions, he also states that each religion has its unique potential, its specific qualities. Yet all religious traditions have the same purpose—to foster true happiness. How to lead a life beyond dogma? "You must keep your mind happy and know how to laugh!"

Part Five, "Interdependence and Emptiness," contains his subtle and technical reflections on queries put to him during a meeting with scientists and philosophers. Here he uses the vast resources of Buddhist philosophy and logic, combined with his considerable knowledge of Western technology, to probe deeply into the mystery of our being in the universe. At its core, reality is paradoxical—both Buddhists and quantum physicists agree on this. But how do the laws of physics and the most esoteric insights of yogis complement each other, and in what way is consciousness part of the ultimate structure of the universe?

Citing observations culled from fundamental Buddhist teachings, he explains how the energies of interdependence are the manifest display of a deep wisdom, devoid of all limits or bias. Thus, at its most esoteric core, reality is truly beyond dogma, devoid of any essence which can be hoarded. This is good news. Complete openness gives us reason for hope, for no matter how often we become distracted from the luminous source, knowledge of this empty openness is always available. This luminosity pulses continuously as the display of compassion. It is present in all life forms, and in all minds, and can be known by philosopher, scientist, and saint.

Beyond Dogma embodies a universal message. In these times of spiritual starvation, these dialogues and discourses provide a sense of being nourished by a living presence whose sole concern is to communicate a message of hope and kindness. With gentle good humor, His Holiness has dedicated his life's work to bringing encouragement and knowledge to all who seek contentment and happiness.

Steven D. Goodman
Institute of Buddhist Studies
Berkeley, California
May, 1996

PART I

REFLECTIONS
ON THE MILLENNIUM

I SEE A FEW FAMILIAR FACES, but this is the first time I have met most of you. I don't think that is terribly important, for wherever I go, I always feel that I am meeting human beings like myself. We can see right away that we are human beings, particularly when a face lights up with the sincerity of a smile, expressing the importance of human feeling. I have found this sincere feeling on many faces, and I am happy to share it with you. This friendly feeling is always present in my mind, along with the knowledge of the oneness of humanity. This attitude is very important because it allows us to identify and share others' problems and suffering.

Even if we consider humanity as a whole we can, of course, find numerous factors that divide us, such as religious faith, customs, language, and culture. Although such diversity is also a source of enrichment for all of us, we must not overemphasize it to the detriment of the wholeness of humanity, or we risk encountering numerous useless problems.

Now, more than ever, in a world where demographic growth and the progress of communication have put us in very close contact with our neighbors, the very survival of humanity depends on our interrelation. That is why, more than ever, we must look on humanity as one entity. The problems we face at the moment go beyond individuals and nations. We can only resolve them through an effort of shared responsibility.

Our mental attitude is totally inadequate, given the urgency of what is needed. We must therefore have a better grasp of reality and make certain that our mental attitude, our lifestyle, and our activities correspond to that reality.

THOUGHTS ON TODAY'S SOCIETY
AND THE FUTURE OF THE WORLD

Your Holiness, you have the rare privilege of being familiar with both the West and the East, the so-called affluent societies and more traditional societies. Both are actually in the midst of an unprecedented moral crisis. We would like to hear your opinion on this subject and benefit from your advice. We would also like to know your feelings regarding the future of the planet. First, however, so that we might better follow your train of thought, we would appreciate it if you would outline the essential elements of Buddhist philosophy for us.

I do not claim to be able to give advice which would help those in difficulty to find an immediate solution to their mental suffering, or any other kind of suffering. I, too, find on occasion that my mind is troubled or confused, or I encounter internal difficulties that I must contend with. Nevertheless, I think it will be very useful for us to share our different points of view and our diverse personal experiences.

It is my habit to emphasize the importance of happiness and satisfaction—these are, I believe, the very purpose of human existence. For example, someone who sets off on a spiritual journey at the cost of great effort and extreme difficulties does not do so with the simple purpose of becoming a martyr, but rather in the hope of eventually attaining lasting happiness. In order to reach this essential goal, he might neglect his present well-being. In my opinion, the way in which we think is very important in the quest for happiness. It is obvious that our mental attitude is one of the prime factors involved in our quest for happiness.

Reflection and logical analysis enable us to develop a more correct way of thinking. The more open our minds are, the more expansive and relaxed, the easier it is to have an accurate view of things. There are two advantages to this. If we keep our mind open, we will remain serene and at ease with ourselves. And the more far-reaching our vision is, the easier it will be to find solutions to problems and difficulties.

As we are all human beings living on earth among countless other human beings, our happiness is intimately connected to that of others. It is hard to imagine personal happiness detached or separate from the happiness of others. For it is certain that if we aspire to happiness, we must be deeply concerned about the happiness of all humankind. This is why I always stress the importance for the future of developing a universal sense of responsibility.

In our religions and in our prayers we often speak of "the wellbeing of all humankind" or "the happiness of humanity." But when I speak of the necessity for universal responsibility, I am not referring to a religious ideal alone, but to action, to participation in such a reality.

Great transformations have, of course, changed our world, particularly where communication among people is concerned. For example, let us consider Tibet and the peoples of the Himalayan region. There was a time when it was possible to live high up in the mountains and remain self-contained. But because of changes around the world, this situation is no longer possible. Even if we wanted to remain isolated, cut off from the rest of the world, we could not.

Think for a moment now of the aspect of economic development. It is inconceivable nowadays for a nation or a continent to live in complete autocracy. Clearly, not only single nations but entire continents depend on each other economically.

Regarding the exchange of knowledge and information, distance is hardly an obstacle anymore; communication around the planet has become virtually instantaneous. When I was young, India and China seemed very far away because it took months to get there. Nowadays, to go from India to Europe or from Europe to America is merely a matter of a few hours. Of course these journeys by airplane are tiring, but that doesn't alter the fact that the other side of the planet is within arm's reach. The world has become a smaller place and each part of the world depends on every other part. Where the environment is concerned, for example, one nation alone, no matter how powerful, cannot solve massive environmental problems, such as the depletion of the ozone layer.

The reality today is that our globe has become tiny and all people and all countries depend closely upon one another. But our mental and spiritual attitudes have not kept pace with reality and are not in harmony with this increased dependency. Are the borders between countries visible from outer space? Of course not! If we think carefully about the interdependence of all earthly phenomena, our little local problems lose their gravity and naturally we begin to see things globally, in terms of humanity as a whole.

In this context, the idea of "me" and "you" loses its primacy. When we realize this fact, this thought spontaneously brings about a deep feeling of responsibility for the common good. Therefore, the more we become involved in the affairs of the world in general, the calmer and happier we will feel in our private lives. In fact, the more we care for others and feel concern for their well-being, the less we will be inclined toward jealousy, pride, or malice. Without a doubt, it is such feelings as these, along with the spirit of competition, that make us more unhappy with each passing day. But if we concern ourselves with the well-being of all, we quite naturally find a feeling of great inner peace.

Only recently the world was still divided into two blocs, one in the East and the other in the West. This division was based less on economic factors than on politics and ideology. As long as nuclear weapons were directed from each side toward the other, one could not help but have a vision of the world based on the ever-present reality of the idea of "me" and "you," "us" and "them." The world was divided by ideology and power. Both sides were prepared to risk a nuclear holocaust to defend themselves, and each aimed their nuclear weapons at the other. Under such circumstances, we are obliged to think in terms of ourselves and others. This era may now be over and we can envision a new world order.

When I met President Bush several years ago, I told him that this new world order would be an excellent thing, provided it was accompanied by compassion. If it did not include compassion, I doubted it could be a success. I think we have come to a very propitious and important moment in the history of our world. We now have the opportunity to work together for the good of humanity.

When one thinks of universal responsibility and tries to have a long-term view of things, birth control becomes essential. From a Buddhist point of view, human existence is very precious. It is not right, therefore, to prevent a birth. But we are now confronted with an excess of precious lives, with far too large a world population. When it comes down to choosing between the survival of humankind as a whole and a few potential human births, the necessity for implementing birth control becomes obvious. But I must insist that birth control be exercised in a nonviolent fashion.

Because of the changes in the world, nuclear weapons have been reduced and even destroyed—a wonderful thing. Disarmament is essential. All existing weapons must be reduced, one after the other, conventional weaponry as well as chemical and nuclear weaponry. It is true that to cease production of arms will likely cause serious economic and industrial problems. But to give up because of such difficulties is not worthy of our humanity, while seeking a solution to this quandary is.

Different religious traditions are an important part of our world, and I believe that religious pluralism is necessary. It is true that different religions express different metaphysical viewpoints, but it is also clear that at least among the major religions, the fundamental message is the same. Favorable conditions do exist, therefore, to learn to live in harmony and work together.

The Cold War is a thing of the past and there is no longer any opposition between the countries of East and West. But a significant gap in economic development between North and South remains. This considerable economic disparity creates enormous problems for the developed countries. The difference in the standard of living is not only unacceptable from a moral point of view, it also creates serious problems in the developed countries as a result of the emigration of workers from Africa, the Middle East, and the Far East who come to France or Germany, for example, to find work.

Among the various solutions that might be imagined, however, to refuse immigration or attempt to deport immigrants are untenable. Moreover, such an attitude offers no long-term solution. A better method would be to create jobs in the countries of origin in order to encourage an increase in the economic standard of living among the local population, who would then no longer need to emigrate to find relative prosperity elsewhere.

To be sure, countries of the former Communist bloc are now confronted with great difficulties, but I believe they have more potential to succeed economically than some other countries. The same applies for countries of the Far East, China, or India. I believe the most difficult case is that of Africa, a vast continent that must contend with enormous difficulties. Not long ago I went to Gabon and visited the place where Albert Schweitzer had lived. Schweitzer was a Frenchman and a great man who showed extraordinary courage helping those who were in poverty and need. If the gap between North and South is to be reduced, it is the people of the South above all who must make a major effort. Wealthy countries can offer their assistance, but the populations of the poorer countries must take responsibility for their own destinies.

Another extremely regrettable and unfortunate state of affairs is that at the very heart of these developing countries there is a great divide. An elite consisting of only a very small number of people control all the country's resources, while the immense majority of the population remain totally dispossessed. I feel deep regret over this. I am not a specialist on African issues, but what was immediately apparent to me during my visit there was that a fundamental need for education exists. I was also struck by how the population of a single country is fragmented into a multitude of ethnic groups, tribes, and languages. This creates a host of problems for which I feel incapable of offering any solutions. Faced with so many apparently insoluble difficulties, one feels almost tempted to implore the protection of Buddha!

Where international affairs are concerned, I often say to my friends: "You live in democratic countries and consider the exercise of democracy within your country as precious and essential, as no doubt it is.

But however much importance you might attach to it where your internal affairs are concerned, you rarely do the same in your international relations!"

Certain scientific thinkers have suggested that there is no need anymore to distinguish between internal and foreign affairs; that we are all equal now, members of one and the same family, and that, in fact, the affairs of the entire world are now "internal" affairs. I find this vision very vast and noble. The adoption of such an attitude will facilitate our task at hand, which is to resolve our common difficulties.

When we talk about providing aid to Third World countries, we impose all sorts of conditions or restrictions that limit it. Our perception is restricted because priority is given to national interests, and this in turn creates a host of obstacles that hinder the smooth functioning of nations among themselves. Such limited vision must be eliminated, and a major factor involved is political will. For political will to achieve its goal, it must be founded on humanitarian feelings and very solid moral principles—those of altruism and a desire to provide genuine well-being to all people and to relieve their suffering.

If political will is underscored by principles such as these, I believe it can be a very powerful tool. Politicians do not drop out of the sky. They are not born in space, but are the product of society, like ourselves. If the entire population possesses moral and ethical values that are just and noble, the politicians produced by that society will quite naturally respect those same values, for they themselves will have developed them. If, on the other hand, a society on the whole is morally corrupt and its members do not respect the ethics of their own lives, they undoubtedly are unjust in criticizing their politicians.

Some people automatically associate morality and principles such as altruism with a religious vision of the world. Such logic implies that those who practice a religion are observing a certain moral code, and that those who do not practice a religion hold that moral principles are useless and are of no interest. I believe it is a great mistake to believe that morality is merely an attribute of religion. One can envision two types of spirituality: the first is tied to religion, while the second is born spontaneously in a human being, and is expressed simply by the love for our neighbor and the desire to do good for them. This is also spirituality. The practice of religion is a good thing, but people also have a right to live without religion. However, without that quality basic to human beings, without that secular spirituality, the individual cannot be happy within himself and risks doing harm to the society to which he belongs.

How can we define this fundamental quality? I would say it is the tenderness and affection found in every human being. This natural love is present from the very first day of our existence. You have only to watch a mother nursing her child: her natural love is obvious; without it she would not offer her breast, perhaps she would not even have any milk. As for the child, it is naturally drawn to the mother's breast, and is moved by spontaneous tenderness and affection for the mother; without these he or she would surely not seek nourishment.

So at the very beginning of life we display the tenderness and affection which are at the very core of human nature. No religious guides have instructed us in that love, no laws have imposed it, no schools have taught it. Love appeared along with our body at birth. It is an inborn trait of all human beings. Since the first day, our life is already marked by this aspect of love for others, and it is essential to preserve this fundamental nature of humankind throughout our existence.

This is also why I maintain the conviction that human nature is basically affectionate and good. If our behavior follows our kind and loving nature, then, quite naturally, immense benefits will result, not only for oneself but also for the society to which we belong. I generally qualify this love and affection as a universal religion. Everyone needs it, believers as much as non-believers. This attitude constitutes the very basis of morality.

If you agree with what I have said about this altruistic love, try to make it a part of yourself as much as possible. On the other hand, if you think differently about it, you can get angry as often as you like—it doesn't matter, everyone is free!

Thank you very much, that is all I have to say.

His Holiness's remarks make us aware of how important humanist thought can be. As a doctor, I have prepared a series of questions which might further the discussion about the biological and spiritual future of humankind. Obviously I have drawn these questions up in the context of the predominantly monotheistic religions of the West—Judaism, Christianity, or Islam.

Recent advances in medicine, biology, and genetics have made possible the infinite replication of the same biological object—that is, the reproduction of living beings endowed with the same physical and intellectual characteristics—and whose behavior can be predetermined. In the future we can expect to influence our own posterity through assisted procreation, which will determine the number and characteristics of individuals. For many years the animal embryo and perhaps the human fetus will be ground for experimentation.

Regarding such experimentation—which is receiving a great deal of coverage from the media—when does His Holiness believe that the fertilized object is endowed with any spiritual or divine sign of life?

Buddhism holds that consciousness penetrates a being at the very moment of conception, and that consequently the embryo is already a living being. This is why we consider abortion to be the same as taking the life of a living being and as such is not a just action. That is what I meant when I spoke of the necessity for nonviolent birth control. However, there can be exceptional situations. I am thinking, for example, of a case where it is certain that the child will be born with abnormalities or where the mother's life is in danger. I am, of course, expressing the Buddhist point of view. In any action one must always consider the good and the bad, the advantages and the disadvantages. Basically, it will all depend upon the intention and motivation behind the action.

What about genetic manipulation, which is a very real prospect—by changing the rules of the human condition, is humanity going against divine will?

One could go along with the idea of genetic manipulation to improve the human body, the brain, for example, and so forth.

Buddhism does not entertain the notion of a God of creation, so this problem is treated under another realm, that of karma—actions from former lives, and the consequences of those actions. If a person is subjected today to genetic manipulation, it is because of acts he committed in the past. Once we acknowledge this series of causes and effects, we have to take into account principally what good and evil can arise as a result of such manipulation. Does it, for example, offer positive therapeutic results?

Then there is the following problem: in order to know whether something is good for humanity or not, it is necessary to experiment with it. In carrying out such experimentation, we are playing with human life. This is indeed a complex problem, difficult to solve. Experimentation with animals gives rise to the same considerations and is equally difficult for Buddhists to accept.

The study of genetics aims to reduce the number of illnesses and human suffering. If, according to His Holiness, suffering is inexorably part of the human condition, might we hope that efforts on the part of human beings will eliminate suffering?

It is difficult to say. But first I would like to ask you something: do you think that genetic manipulation might one day make human beings immortal? I think it would be very difficult.

First of all, I'm not sure it's something to strive for.

Should we not? I really don't know. Imagine that it were possible. After a certain time any further births would have to be prevented, or there would be a serious demographic problem. On the other hand, if we were thus able to put an end to new births as well as to death, we would be setting up an equilibrium which we would have to maintain; failing to do so would lead to catastrophe.

Allow me to rephrase my question. In monotheistic religious philosophies, suffering is often perceived as a means to salvation. What is the position of Buddhism in this regard?

I think that the position of Buddhism is similar. Through observation and reflection on the suffering of human beings, the desire to be liberated from suffering will arise.

Your Holiness, I would like to ask you a question about relations between China and Tibet. You seem confident that the West will put pressure on China. Do you really believe that the West would jeopardize a market of a billion consumers in order to defend the autonomy of a few million Tibetans? Would it not be more important and, in the long run, more effective to develop your spiritual influence in China itself, rather than remain in opposition to that country? Also, do you think that the economic evolution of China is compatible with the survival of its political system? Do you think that Tibetan values will resist economic progress brought by China? Isn't the development of the Chinese economy the greatest danger to Tibet?

For fourteen years we have been trying very seriously to negotiate with China on the Tibetan question, but even after making many concessions our efforts have been in vain. It has become clear, therefore, that pressure on China from the international community is indispensable. Our own experience has shown that our efforts have yielded no concrete results; hence the importance of such worldwide pressure. That does not mean, however, that we are handing everything over to others.

The reason we choose to follow a nonviolent path, despite considerable criticism, is that in the end the solution must be found between Tibetans and Chinese. Such a solution can only be worked out between our two countries directly. The support of the Chinese people, in particular Chinese intellectuals, is therefore essential. This is why we have adopted a nonviolent stance from the very start, despite all the difficulties. In this way more and more Chinese people, both in China and abroad, are beginning to take an interest in and show sympathy for our cause. Some have even thanked us for having chosen this path. In any case, the choice of the path of negotiation toward resolution of the problem is, for me, a spiritual act.

For nearly fourteen years, we have been witnessing considerable economic development in China, thanks to a liberalization of the economic system. However, on the political level there has not been the slightest liberalization, not the slightest improvement. I think that in the long run economic liberalization in China may lead to political liberalization as well; it is possible.

The way things stand at the moment, one could say that Chinese society is made up, roughly, of three categories. There are, first of all, the leaders and those faithful to the Communist party; then there are the intellectuals and students; and finally, the masses. If we analyze what interests each category we come to see that for the first category it is power and control over the country. The Communist party leaders want to remain in power at any price and do not hesitate to use any means at their disposal to do so. They have shown quite clearly what they are capable of at Tiananmen Square.

The second category is the influential minority of the country which will, in the end, establish democracy there. As for the third category, the people—they are more concerned with everyday life, with their standard of living, how to find food, housing, a bicycle, or perhaps a motorcycle, a refrigerator, or even a washing machine. I don't think they are concerned about whether the country will become democratic or not. Economic development has given confidence to the first and third groups, and the third may be content with that. But the second group is isolated and at a disadvantage, and there is a risk they may become demoralized. If that were the case it would be a disaster, not only for a billion Chinese but also for the entire planet.

Look at China: it is the most populated country on earth. The Chinese people live under the yoke of a totalitarian system and an ideology that glorifies the machinery of war. Moreover, China has nuclear weapons. If the economy continues to develop under the same circumstances, I think we might see some very severe consequences, not only for bordering countries like Tibet, but also for a large country like India, and ultimately the entire planet.

To respond to the second part of your question, I do not think that economic development per se is necessarily a threat to the culture and spirituality of Tibet, if, in its implementation, it takes into account the preexisting conditions in the country. Economic development may coincide with cultural development. When we speak of happiness in Buddhism, this also implies material well-being.

Where we are concerned, China's economic development raises the serious question of the colonization of Tibet by bringing in a large number of Chinese. The greatest threat for Tibet is that of a transfer of population, of massive Chinese immigration. The influx of Chinese colonists has created an atmosphere of extreme tension all over Tibet, which gives rise to continual human rights violations. In addition, it is causing considerable damage to the environment. Whether it is deliberate or not, a sort of cultural genocide is taking place in Tibet and this is the most grave danger for the future of the country.

You said on a recent broadcast that you still felt like a Marxist. What exactly did you mean by that? You have in many ways a great faith in democracy, since you intend to abandon political power in an autonomous Tibet. What in your opinion is the existing type of democracy closest to Buddhist values? Is there not a certain contradiction between those values and the rules of a democracy?

I find certain aspects of Marxism most praiseworthy from an ethical point of view, principally in its treatment of material equality and the defense of the poor against exploitation by a minority. These aspects are quite acceptable. I believe one might say that the economic system closest to Buddhism, and more particularly to the Great Vehicle, would be a socialist economic system. Marxism is based on very noble ideas, such as the defense of the rights of those who are most disadvantaged. But the energy given to the application of these principles is rooted in a violent hatred for the ruling classes, and that hatred is channeled into class struggle and the destruction of the exploiting class. Once the ruling class is eliminated, there is nothing left to offer the people and everyone is reduced to a state of poverty. Why should this be so? Because there is a total absence of compassion from the start.

Regarding the future of Tibet, it has already been decided that it will be a democracy. I do not know of any contradictions between democracy and Buddhism. I would even go on to say that Mahayana Buddhism is the religion of democracy. Let me give you an example. We say that a monastic community (Sanskrit: *sangha*) exists when a group of four monks is formed. When there is an important decision to be taken, the group of monks as a whole must resolve the question and not just the one who heads the group. For the future of Tibet I would say that the ideal would be a mixed economy. If you question me any further on what type of economy I would advocate, I think my answer might be very brief!

I would like to ask you a question regarding the relations between North and South which you have already spoken of at length in your previous response. Given the fact that in France and in the Western world 80 percent of Western aid granted to developing countries is lost through corruption, what type of relations would you like to see between the industrialized nations and the Third World?

I believe I did touch on this question when I said that it was necessary to reduce the gap between the nations of the North and those of the South. The very first thing to do is to reduce the gap between the elite of the developing countries and the general population. As I said earlier, above all the countries themselves must make the effort to progress. That is obvious. Aside from that, to stand there all the time with one's hand outstretched is no solution. We Tibetans have received considerable aid during our exile. In the beginning we relied heavily upon that aid. Having said that, we also, above all, exerted a great effort ourselves to insure our survival. And now, not only do we meet our own needs but we are also working on all kinds of projects to preserve the identity and culture of Tibet.

Therefore, the effort must above all be made by the Third World countries themselves. At present these countries are presided over by an elite class, generally educated in the West, and the gap between them and the general population is considerable. I think, therefore, that the first essential step to reduce these disparities is to educate the people, which would enable the disadvantaged classes to raise themselves to a higher level of knowledge.

During my visit to Gabon I said to my African hosts that they lived on an immense continent with a wealth of history, enormous potential, and vast reserves of natural resources, but that they lacked confidence in themselves. That confidence must be developed, great determination must be fostered, and then every effort must be made to bring about a real transformation of the present situation. Look at Mahatma Gandhi: even though he had a very high level of Western education he never forgot or estranged himself from his own culture.

INTERDEPENDENCE AND THE SPIRIT OF ENLIGHTENMENT

Could you tell us, in a few words, what Buddhism is? We often wonder whether it is a philosophy or a religion; it is often reduced in the West to the notion of reincarnation, but without doubt it is much more than that.

To answer your first question, I generally say that the essence of Buddhism, from the point of view of personal conduct, is nonviolence; from a philosophical point of view it is the interdependence of all phenomena. As an illustration of nonviolence I would say that the ideal conduct is to do good for others. If that turns out to be difficult, then at least we must avoid causing harm.

As for the view of the interdependence of phenomena, this refers to the fact that all phenomena depend upon the different causes and conditions producing them, or that all phenomena exist in relation to each other and depend upon each other. The concept of interdependence enables us to understand how our happiness and our suffering appear only in the presence of causes and conditions, and how their very existence depends upon a number of factors. This understanding will lead us to nonviolent action.

From the point of view of conduct—nonviolence—we can say that Buddhism is a religion, whereas when we consider the concept of the interdependence of phenomena, we can say that Buddhism is a philosophy. But in the strictest sense, the term "religion" presupposes belief in a Creator God. In that case, Buddhism does not correspond to the definition of a religion. Certain Western scholars suggest that Buddhism is not a religion but rather a science of the mind. Nevertheless, a large part of Buddhism is devoted to meditation. We are told how, through meditation, we can progress along the Way and reach ever-higher spiritual levels, what we call the ground and the path. In this respect, Buddhism is indisputably a religion.

There are, all over the world, religions in which faith is the principal element; at the other extreme are the radical materialists. Both approaches are far removed from each other; Buddhists are found somewhere in the middle. According to those religions based essentially on faith, Buddhism is not a religion. However, we cannot identify it with pure materialism, either. For this reason, Buddhism can bridge the two approaches.

Reincarnation is part of the teachings that are at the basis of Buddhism. Through meditation on these basic truths, we can progress along the spiritual path and attain realization. Indeed, we could not obtain a spiritual realization by meditating on basic ideas that are erroneous or nonexistent. For example, emptiness does exist, basically. That is why we can meditate on it. The same thing applies for the impermanence of phenomena and suffering. It is because they exist that we can meditate on them and, therefore, bring about spiritual realization. If these things did not exist, this would not be possible. The principle of former and future lives, and therefore of reincarnation, is one of the basic tenets of Buddhism.

Does the way you dress have any religious significance? Does the fact of having an arm bared have religious significance?

It's for developing the arm muscles! The Buddhist monastic robe came from India. Because India is a hot country, monks not only had bare arms but also a bare chest, except for the shawl they wore. I believe in Cambodia the monks wear long sleeves under their saffron robes because of the cold. In Tibet, despite the cold, it is not customary to wear sleeves. A large thick shawl is worn instead. I ought to mention that the monastic robes are made up of several pieces of cloth sewn together. They are assembled from different pieces of cloth in order to avoid a feeling of attachment for clothing. Despite that, once the pieces are put together it sometimes happens that we grow attached to them all the same!

Your Holiness, you said that Buddhist philosophy is based on the interdependence between phenomena and human beings. Is Buddhism therefore better situated to understand the demands of present-day ecology?

The view of existence in dependence and of the interdependent origins of phenomena can both help. Where interdependence is concerned, if we are to assure future happiness, it is necessary to create the causes of happiness now. Consequently, today's generation must consider the environment not only for their own good, but also for the good of many future generations. From the point of view of existence in dependence, the state of the environment will for a large part determine the state of our health. If the air that we breathe is not pure, there is a risk that we will suffer the consequences. Thus, the view on the relation between cause and effect as well as the view on the mutual dependence of phenomena are both very important. The view of interdependence contributes in particular to a holistic or global worldview.

Humankind has, from its beginnings, debated the question of an ideal society. Might the pre-1959 Tibetan society of before the Chinese invasion be considered an ideal society?

The old Tibetan society was not perfect. It was a society of farming and grazing based largely on serfdom. Yet if we compare it to that of

India or China at the same time, it was not as hard and it was more compassionate. I believe a number of ancient civilizations, like those of the American Indians, had a great respect for the earth, for nature, for trees. In the Tibetan culture, our relations with nature, including animals, were very peaceful. We lived in great harmony with nature. At its foundation and thereafter, after the arrival of Buddhism in Tibet, Tibetan society in general was characterized by compassion and openness. It was a society where people felt at ease. For those reasons I believe it might serve as an example.

More than speech which expresses thought, might not the distinctive feature of humanity be silence?

For those who have set out on a spiritual and contemplative path, and who practice meditation, silence plays an important part. For those who follow no spiritual path, who are non-believers, the simple fact of remaining silent can be very restful and relaxing.

Don't you think that there are many people who may seem to be adults, if for no other reason than their age, but who are actually like children precisely because they do not practice meditation?

I think there are a number of ways to define maturity. Age, for a start, and then the way one thinks, the development of one's qualities, then finally experience and spiritual realization. There are thus three ways of looking at what constitutes maturity. Having said that, there are elderly people who still have a childish spirit and others who, although very young, show great maturity in the way they think.

How do you explain that increasing numbers of young people in the West are turning to Eastern wisdom and spirituality, when the West also has a rich tradition?

Most Western countries have a very old Christian civilization. I don't think that this situation is about to change, and that is a good thing.

Nevertheless, there are millions of human beings and among these millions there are bound to be a great variety of interests, natures, and spiritual dispositions. So among them there will be those who are attracted to Buddhism—just as in Tibet, which has been Buddhist for centuries, there are also Muslims and Christians. It is normal that certain Westerners be interested in Buddhism, now and in the future. Among them, some are interested in logical reasoning or meditation and are attracted by the richness of Buddhism in those realms. Some people are drawn to the possibility of waking up with three eyes instead of two after undergoing surgery!

Do you think that the role of higher education is simply to prepare minds for scientific disciplines and that teachers have no other role than to dispense knowledge? Do they have a higher mission?

A very good question! The fundamental distinction of humankind—which makes for the superiority of human beings over other species—is our great intelligence. This intelligence means that society is filled with a great diversity of views, all different from each other, and all conducive to a great variety of types of behavior. This can lead to extremely complex situations, sometimes to problems.

Let us take the case of a single individual. He can change his set way of thinking, thus creating internal conflict. I often joke in saying that without contradictions, without internal conflict, a person is not really a human being. But at the same time it is due to this intelligence that we can overcome our contradictions, resolve our conflicts, and find solutions. Human intelligence is both the source and the solution to all our problems. Education—access to knowledge—develops and stimulates this intelligence. But it is by no means certain that it is a source of good only. It can do harm by creating other problems.

Education in itself is neither positive nor negative. That is why, in order to elevate and direct human intelligence toward the good, it is important that educators be courageous, sincere, and honest. Whether this means parents within the family, or teachers in schools and universities, educators must not be content with merely transmitting information, but must also try to help the student live well, to be content in their private life and useful in society. To do this they must feel concerned about the future of their students and encourage them. It is therefore indispensable that the acquisition of knowledge go hand-in-hand with the development of altruism.

I am sure you are aware that in our country many young people are afflicted with AIDS, that many of them take drugs, and that the number of suicides among young people is increasing. Do you have any suggestions for the leaders of this country to help find remedies for these terrible problems?

The primary method to overcome social afflictions is self-discipline in personal life, through which one attempts to master self-control; it is very difficult to impose discipline from the outside. To explain the benefits of personal discipline, let us take the example of the villages on the slopes of the Himalayas. Indian authorities, policemen, and other people have often told me that in years gone by there was little crime, few thefts or fights, almost no lying, and that in spite of the absence of material progress and modern education, people were very honest. But over the years, as education and other elements of modern civilization reached the villages from the plains below, crime began to increase. When everyone practices self-control through internal discipline, there is no crime despite the absence of policemen in the world outside. This demonstrates the importance of self-discipline.

But one must understand that what we mean by that is not simply the systematic repression of all desires or aspirations that might come to mind. As I've just pointed out, reliable and genuine discipline comes not from repression, but from an understanding of all the whys and wherefores of our acts. We may get a certain momentary satisfaction from following our impulses; however, we must also be aware of the consequences, which may not be immediately apparent, but which will not fail to show up in the future. Let us therefore use our intelligence and wisdom to restrain our momentary desires and to weigh the good and bad effects of our actions, in order to determine the best path to follow.

Take, for example, those who indulge in sexual misconduct or drug abuse. What induces someone to behave in such a way? An instant of pleasure. But if you compare that momentary pleasure with the ultimate consequences of your actions, it becomes obvious that immediate satisfaction cannot hold up against the negative long-term consequences. It is therefore essential to be aware of our actions and their consequences. Faith, of course, is necessary, but education is even more important. The entire community must be responsible, not just the authorities. In order to build a healthy society, each member of that society must share the responsibility.

What is your opinion regarding the use of condoms?

Very good, a good choice. However, I have a better solution to offer for birth control and the prevention of AIDS: celibacy, chastity! May there be many monks and nuns! And if that proves to be too difficult or impossible, then the best solution is the one you mentioned.

Your Holiness, your words a moment ago resonated with praise of nature, but I believe there is another environment, a hostile one, that of human beings. Concerning those who are dispossessed, in exile, or homeless, do you have an opinion on the responsibility of the state regarding these unfortunately all-too-common experiences?

When we talk about government, and the government in question is one democratically elected by the people, in the final analysis the people are the true leaders. They choose a government which then has the responsibility of fulfilling its obligations. Clearly, once elected, the government is responsible for all its citizens, particularly those who are weaker and more disadvantaged. This is for moral reasons as well as practical ones. If a breach is created among the different social classes, problems will arise. My personal opinion, as well as that of a number of my Buddhist friends, both laypeople and clerics, is that the ideal economic system would be of a socialist type.

That answers the question on the level of the state. Could you now, with regard to what I will call international law, outline those principles that would define the duties and the obligations on an international basis, which might, in time, lead to an agreement as to what humanity could aspire to as a whole?

Whether talking about individuals or governments, the principle that must guide us is that of human rights. If we live in a country where human rights exist and are respected, we are naturally responsible for our duties and responsibilities. How nice it would be if we could enjoy human rights without assuming the responsibilities they entail! But unfortunately that hardly seems possible. Of course, I think the most important thing is to have a sense of responsibility and commitment, of concern for others, for each one of our fellow human beings. This seems a fundamental thing to me, but I am not an expert on international relations, or on international law among independent nations. However, I have a deep personal conviction that on both an individual and governmental level, it is absolutely indispensable to have a sense of universal responsibility and to feel concern for other people.

I would like to add a few words regarding this notion of universal responsibility. When we feel responsible, concerned, and committed, we begin to feel deep emotion and great courage. This emotion does not appear spontaneously, without direct cause; it is the product of prolonged reflection and intense logical analysis. It is a healthy emotion. This deep-rooted feeling is quite distinct from the daily emotions which suddenly spring to mind for no particular reason, without any deep-rooted justification. I am referring to the random emotions we experience at any moment of the day, which come to trouble our minds and which, far from strengthening our spirit, destroy our peace of mind.

Of course we all know what emotions are. But if we can nurture those emotions based on reason, we will no longer be disturbed by fleeting and insignificant ones. Take, for example, someone who in their family environment is constantly plagued by all kinds of irritations, by the minor details of everyday life. By broadening his outlook to encompass first the nation and then humanity as a whole, by learning to make his thinking both serious and rational, that same person could gradually develop a sense of universal responsibility. In so doing there is a good chance he would be less prone to anger over everyday worries.

In Buddhism we have the concept of *bodhichitta,* the spirit of enlightenment. This denotes an aspiration to realize Buddhahood in order to bring about good for all beings, and it is equivalent to the notion of universal responsibility. From my own personal experience, it is a great help to think about the spirit of enlightenment when we are sad or our mind is disturbed. If we think about taking on a great responsibility when we are troubled or confused, our mind opens, relaxes, and becomes stronger. On the one hand, by developing this notion of universal responsibility we take a lot upon ourselves. But the end result is that we are happier.

Your Holiness, currently in the West the public discussion of words such as "religion," "ethics," and "morals" signals a need for rules of conduct. In every field there is such a need; we talk of the ethics of politicians, of business, of biology and medicine, of journalism. Ethics have certainly made a strong comeback. What do you think of this evolution? How can it be explained? Why is it happening?

I think that this evolution is the fruit of experience. After encountering enormous problems and great difficulties, we come to realize the necessity of a moral code.

More precisely, in France, Germany, and the United States there is much discussion about a business ethic. Can the two terms—ethics and business—be reconciled? Aren't money and moral considerations mutually exclusive? Some people consider an ethic to be a way to manage a business, for better internal control where salaries are concerned, or in its relations with the outside world. Do you think that this is a devaluation of the very notion of an ethic?

First of all, you must understand what is meant by an ethic. We can distinguish two types. The first is associated with a religion; we choose to follow a spiritual path and we observe the moral codes laid down by that religion. The second is that which applies to people who have no religion but who nevertheless choose spontaneously to subscribe to a certain ethic founded on their experience of searching for happiness. I think that this desire to subscribe to a certain moral code outside of a religious context can be attributed to a basic trait of human nature—affection or human tenderness.

I often explain things this way: there are many professions, many fields of human activity. Business, politics, education, science, technology, medicine, law—all kinds of different activities. If all these professional activities could be based on human feelings such as understanding and the love of our neighbor, they would be more human, more positive, more constructive. It is nevertheless likely that there would still be problems and difficulties, but I think they would be fewer. On the other hand, if these professional activities are completely mechanical, devoid of any human sentiment, they risk causing a great deal of harm.

The same thing applies to religion. If a religion is rooted in human feeling, where each individual is concerned by the happiness of others, it will have a positive effect on all. But a religion practiced without any feeling of humanity, without commitment or compassion, would only create problems.

As for the relation between ethics and business, since all commercial enterprises must take into account competition and profit, the union between them will necessarily be a fragile one, but not impossible. A spirit of competition can be positive, depending on what motivates it. Bad competition is that which tends to take advantage of others, to their detriment; good competition leads to the development and improvement of our activities. I also think that industry has a very particular responsibility where the environment is concerned and that there, too, ethics must be taken into account. Those who participate in business are human beings and, like all human beings, they need affection and human warmth. I think that ethics must be the link between the personal needs of each individual and the needs of the environment.

There is something I find particularly striking, a sort of paradox, which ties in with the preceding question in a way. The development of science and technology and the ever-increasing efficiency of the individual's immediate environment goes hand-in-hand with what seems to be an ever-increasing disorder in society. I question this in order to know whether what we call rationality is not sometimes just the illusion *of rationality. I would like to know your opinion on this matter.*

I do not think our society is really rational. There is reason, and then there is reason. There might be a certain logic appropriate for a given need, for profit, for example, which does not take into account the long-term consequences of related actions. In a broader context, that of the environment, for example, such reasoning would be invalidated and lose importance. It all depends on how we apply our reasoning. Are we narrow- or broad-minded? Are we considering only its specificity, or the global situation as well? Is our view short- or long-term? Are we intellectually short-sighted or clear-eyed?

Is it conceivable that a Buddha be reincarnated in the body of a non-Asian, a non-Tibetan, perhaps a European or an African?

It is possible. According to Buddhism, emanations of Buddhas can be found not only among human beings but also in the animal world.

For too long animals have been treated like objects, used by human beings for food, clothing, transportation, entertainment, and often cruel scientific experiments done solely for human satisfaction. What do you think of the rights and lives of animals?

According to Buddhism the life of all beings—human, animal, or otherwise—is precious, and all have the same right to happiness. For this reason I find it disgraceful that animals are used without being shown the slightest compassion, and that they are used for scientific experiments. Even if you do not look at this from a religious point of view, it is certain that birds, wild animals—all the creatures inhabiting our planet—are our companions. They are a part of our world, we share it with them. I think that if animals came one day to disappear from the surface of the globe everyone would be deeply sorry. I have also noticed that those who lack any compassion for animals and who do not hesitate to kill them are also those who, sooner or later, show a lack of compassion toward human beings. Inversely, the more compassion we have toward animals, the more we regard their lives as precious, then the more respect we have for human life.

Are Buddhists vegetarians?

I think that from a Buddhist point of view it is very important to be vegetarian. I always say that even if on an individual level one does not always manage to stick to a vegetarian diet, when large numbers of people meet for a party, a conference, or any other gathering, it is indispensable that the group avoids eating meat. As for myself, I have tried my best to introduce vegetarianism to Tibetan society.

While organizing this conference, I had lunch several times with a Buddhist who invited me to a restaurant where they primarily serve meat.

Perhaps he was a nomad Buddhist from the high Tibetan plateau!

Is it necessary to withdraw from society in order to attain spiritual realization?

In general it is preferable for those who practice a religion not to withdraw from society. However—and this is true for all religious traditions—when a person feels that he or she is ready to truly devote themselves to successful meditation, then it is a good thing to go into retreat for a certain length of time.

Buddhism does not worship a God. Who, or what, therefore, are its divinities, and to whom does one devote worship?

Indeed, Buddhism recognizes neither an eternal God nor a Creator God. However, it does allow that ordinary beings proceed progressively along a spiritual path, purifying their minds and developing all the inner qualities, succeeding in this way to attain enlightenment and perfection. These beings are known as *aryabuddhas.* We also accept the existence of superior beings who have traveled the spiritual path up to a certain point; they are called the *aryasangha.* For Buddhists such superior beings exist, and it is to them, Buddhas and bodhisattvas, that we present offerings and petitions. This is done with the goal of ourselves becoming a Buddha. This is why, in agreement with the varying dispositions and needs of individuals, Buddhas appear in a great variety of forms. Their emanations are called deities.

Do you think that the young Tibetans of tomorrow will have the same will to preserve their Tibetan identity when confronted with the lure of consumer society?

I have noticed that, in general, the many Tibetans now dispersed throughout the world, even those who live in the consumer societies of the West, still have a great desire to preserve their culture and their traditions. But of course there is still a risk.

For people who suffer from chronic illness, for young eighteen-year-olds stricken with AIDS, what can be done to help them endure, to ease their suffering?

It all depends on where we stand with regard to our suffering. If indeed we are left to ourselves without any inner alternatives, the suffering will be what it is, pain will be what it is, and it will be difficult to escape. If, on the other hand, we have trained ourselves to think in a certain way, then when we encounter such difficulties we will be better able to understand them and endure them. We will know how to deflect our thoughts toward suffering greater than our own, in order to make our own seem relatively less.

A Buddhist who suffers from AIDS or some other very painful disease might think about actions and their consequences. He might formulate the wish that his present experience of pain resulting from past negative actions helps to eliminate all the dormant pain still within him. He might also conceive the idea of giving his happiness to all beings and through his own suffering assume the suffering of others. He might also see in his illness the chance to better understand all the serious defects of his disposition and conclude that they are of the nature of suffering, then think about the disadvantages of cyclic existence (Sanskrit: *samsara*) itself. By expanding his perception of the situation, his suffering will seem that much reduced and will take on less importance. This might then be of some comfort to him.

I would also like to point out that in our society we must at all costs avoid the tendency to shut away those who suffer, those who are dispossessed or diseased, as if they were a burden on society. On the contrary, we must try, with a spirit of kindness, to help these people in particular.

Do you think that the principle of the separation of church and state is necessary for a democracy? Is Buddhism a religion which precludes all fanaticism? If yes, why?

I think that it is important that the church, as an institution, be separate from the state. Where we are concerned, we have already established a constitution which will come into force when Tibet regains its freedom. It has been clearly established that the government will be democratically elected by the people.

I think the danger of fanaticism is quite limited in Buddhism. It actually encompasses a number of philosophical schools such as, among others, the Vaibashika, designed for those who express viewpoints which are progressively broader and deeper. Within one and the same doctrine, we speak of the Small Vehicle and the Great Vehicle, or the *shravaka, pratyekabuddhas,* and bodhisattva paths. These different schools and approaches exist to respond to the varied intellectual capacities of each individual, to the different nature and predisposition of every human being. Since these different philosophical views coexist in harmony within the very heart of Buddhism in order to correspond to the needs of each individual, it is easy for a Buddhist to understand that all the other religions, while they may present different metaphysical and philosophical views, can bring great blessings to human beings in response to their aspirations. For this reason there is little room for fanaticism.

I think we must accept religious pluralism in our relations with different religions. One of the best means to prevent fanaticism is to improve relations among religions.

Your Holiness, one last question on an important subject: what is the role of women in Buddhism in comparison with their position in other religions?

If we look at the rules of the Vinaya (the monastic and lay discipline), women as well as men can be fully ordained, becoming *bhikshu* or *bhikshuni.* However, the Indian context was such that, according to this same Vinaya, a bhikshuni had to sit behind her male counterpart even if she had a longer history of religious life than he did. That is one thing.

But in the Supreme Vehicle of Buddhism, in esoteric Mahayana, special attention is given to the feminine principle, which means that women have an important place. Certain rules of the Vinaya were influenced by the Indian society of the time, in which women's existence was perceived as inferior. The possibility of amending such practices has been raised; there will be a meeting to discuss the matter.

A DESIRE FOR PEACE

Let us talk of peace. Peace is very important. Thanks to the human character, which prefers peace to bloodshed, it is possible to lessen violence and create a more harmonious, peaceful, and caring human society, even if our fundamental nature is sometimes weakened by uncontrolled emotions. There are two types of means to this end: a short- or a long-term strategy.

Regarding the short-term strategy, you are all well on your way to dealing with contemporary problems like violence. Therefore anything I might say would be pointless.

But as for the long-term strategy, our future, I think education is the primary factor which will allow human intelligence to be channeled in the right direction. It might be useful to examine closely the failings of our current educational system. It is obvious, for example, that certain countries deliberately foster negative emotions like hatred of their neighbors. Our present reality shows us that humanity cannot survive without genuine international cooperation, however. Notions such as "my country," "your country," "my religion," "your religion," have become minor. We must, on the contrary, insist on the fact that the other person is as worthy as we are. This is humanity! This is why we must reexamine our educational system.

Now for the media. I respect them very much and I appreciate the fact that they interfere with everyone's business! Some important people do not always behave very honestly. So it is extremely useful to have the media examine them. Journalists are notoriously nosy and do their job well. On the other hand, I reproach them for attaching too much importance to the negative aspects which can greatly discourage the human mind. There should be more balance in what they choose to report. They show us too much misfortune, even though we do have the possibility and the potential to change all of that, thanks to the good, compassionate nature of which I have already spoken. This nature is the deep root of our thoughts and the basis of any potential development. I often find myself contradicting certain people in these terms: "Despite the bad news in the papers, look at all the millions of young, sick, or old people who receive help thanks to compassion or human affection; positive emotions are therefore as active as negative ones."

Religion is sometimes also a source of problems, due to a lack of mutual communication, in my experience. Once we establish good relations our field of vision is enlarged. We discover that we can work on the basis of what we have in common and that we can learn from each other. In this way, I believe, mutual respect can be developed and religious conflicts will be reduced.

And then there are the difficulties that arise because of politicians and national leaders. Of course when dealing with dictatorships or authoritarian regimes, you cannot tell what will happen; these are difficult cases. But the politicians of democratic countries put a great part of their wisdom to use in service to others, and that is very good. When election time is near however, they keep the rest of that wisdom for their voters, and that cannot help but create a certain imbalance. How can the quality of politicians be improved? I really don't know.

All these essential factors must be studied in the long run, very seriously and in greater depth, for they concern humanity as a whole. Each of us is a part of the human family, whatever our social background. Whether you are a teacher, economist, politician, lawyer, member of the clergy, businessperson, or "man-on-the-street," everyone must assume their share of responsibility and use their potential to bring about a world of greater harmony.

At a time when a number of totalitarian regimes have crumbled, deplorable events like those in Bosnia or Africa nevertheless reveal how necessary is has become to do everything possible to prevent such terrible suffering from now on. There is much talk of a "new world order." It is very difficult to change a structure once it has been established. But now that the old structure has fallen, the moment has come to make the most of that change. However, when people don't know what to do, they are often even more anxious. Whatever the case, it is up to the governments to seize the opportunity.

The difficult task of nuclear disarmament remains. For as long as there are such weapons, a disaster is still possible because we are constantly at the mercy of a handful of irresponsible people. As for me, I still advocate what I call inner disarmament through the reduction of hatred and the promotion of compassion. Moreover, by reducing arms, we limit the damage in cases where hostility might break out.

We must of course also consider birth control. The divide between North and South is another source of problems. According to certain specialists, if the countries of the South reached a standard of living comparable to that of the North, the planet's resources would no longer suffice. This is yet another very complex situation.

To conclude, we may ask how human thought might be changed.

Once again, it is up to each of us to try and make an effort. I would therefore like to remind humankind and more specifically those actively involved in the social organizations, of this: human will is fundamental. We can accomplish the most difficult things if we have determination. We will achieve nothing, even the easiest thing, if we take a pessimistic attitude. According to my own experience, determination and confidence are key factors to success.

THE TREE OF PEACE

To all the welcoming inhabitants of this fine country with its rich landscape—I wish to you and your homeland happiness, prosperity, and virtue.

—*inscription in the guest book of the village of Marzens by His Holiness the Fourteenth Dalai Lama*

I am very happy to be together with you this late afternoon to plant a tree of peace. I have been living for a few days on the land of your community, in order to present some of the more profound aspects of Buddhist philosophy. I have found the location and the countryside to be naturally conducive to serenity and tranquility, and these qualities are most favorable for this type of teaching. As I walk around and happen to pass the inhabitants of this place, I see great smiles on their faces which gives me the impression that I am meeting up with old friends. I thank you for this feeling.

I think that in a small village the sense of community life is a much more vital reality than in a large town where it tends to be lost in the crowds. As for me, I think that feeling close to other human beings with a sense of love and tenderness is one of the most essential aspects of the human condition. I believe that if our spirits are turned toward kindness, toward the positive side of things, toward love of our neighbor, we have found the best way to solve our problems. When we are confronted with human problems, trying to solve them by force will not bring a lasting solution. That is why I attach great importance to the feeling of mutual love among all human beings, as well as to the sense of responsibility of community life. Indeed, these concepts of community and human kindness are the source of peace everywhere in the world. They are at the origin of all individual and collective fulfillment in a human community, and therefore they are the concern of us all.

I have heard that this land is very fertile and that the region has always been prosperous. I will pray that this prosperity never ceases to develop, and that the inhabitants continue to live in joy, tranquility, and happiness. May all your aspirations be brought to fruition and may peace reign among all beings. And as for the tree which we have just planted, I will ask my friends to come from time to time to see how it is growing and give me news of it.

HUMANITY AND NATURE

Om Mani Padme Hum! The six syllables of this mantra are intended to dissipate the suffering of the six classes of beings who wander in cyclic existence. This leads us naturally to the understanding that the suffering or happiness of human beings and the condition of the environment, of the world around us, are linked. I thank you for your welcome to this university which, although young, is nonetheless already quite renowned. I am very happy to be here—all the more so for having learned that this site was once a military base and has been transformed into a place of knowledge and learning.

The environment and its protection are now essential issues. This is not merely a question of ethics or morals, but truly one of survival. My interest in environmental issues is not the result of a study I might have undertaken over a period of time; rather, it is something which has come to me in a very surprising manner. You know that in Tibet, wherever you go, you can drink the water. In India and other places, people generally make a distinction between drinking water and other water. That is why I am surprised when people speak of the environment, and why I profess a great interest in it. After consulting specialists on the question I have come to realize that this is undoubtedly a very serious, indeed grave, issue.

The calamities caused by war are immediate and obvious. Where the environment is concerned, the destruction takes place much more slowly. Imperceptible at the onset, it gradually increases, and once it becomes obvious it is often too late. I am very glad and filled with hope to see that the environment has become a source of major concern for everyone. Given our intelligence and our desires, which are part of human nature, we sometimes quite unintentionally indulge in activities which prove very harmful in the long run. However, if properly controlled, that same intelligence can find the means to solve the problems.

This is why I feel that it is very important to be motivated by compassion, or by the perspective of others' suffering and its negative long-term consequences. Generally, if people are motivated by kindness, this will enhance their self-confidence and, in turn, their determination. I believe that this determination is elementary when it is coupled with wisdom or intelligence; inner strength and courage become the essential elements enabling us to overcome any obstacle, whatever it might be. Also, all the technological, demographic, or economic problems arising on a global scale must be made known to everyone, clearly presented. It is by showing concern for what threatens us and by being aware of the urgent need to find solutions that we will be more capable of concentrating our energy in the search for solutions. An institute which studies the environment in a scientific way can provide qualitative and quantitative data to evaluate the evolution and degradation of the environment. A scientific approach of this kind, supported by the media, is fundamental.

Our concern for the environment must not be limited solely to our own region or to the borders of our own country. It is a question which concerns everyone on earth. It is essential that everyone become aware of it, in order to join forces in dealing with the problem. In my opinion, if young people were made aware of environmental issues from their early childhood, they would make such concerns part of their store of knowledge and keep it all their lives.

One of the greatest problems in dealing with the environment is, of course, the modern economy. It is true that the economy must be developed, but there is also the risk that only profit will be taken into account. Of course we are obliged to use the earth's resources, but the danger exists of overexploiting them. Some specialists even go so far as to say we must change the Western way of life. I do not know how realistic that is, but it is certain that everything is interconnected. It is therefore of prime importance to find a middle road, without going to an extreme.

How can we, in the West, reconcile technological progress and our concern for the preservation of the environment? In particular, do you believe that humanity and nature are inseparable or, on the contrary, do you think one might imagine a world from which human beings are absent?

According to Buddhist cosmology, there is indeed a period at the very inception of the universe from which the human species is absent. There will also be, in a distant future, a period where human society will disappear, while the universe will remain for a time. Perhaps then there will be greater peace on earth—who knows! I think that the key factor, as I have already said, is the relation between technology and the protection of the environment. I've been told that recently many factories have been built which are less polluting. For example, when I was in Stockholm, my friends told me that the fish which had disappeared some time before from the river running through town had finally reappeared and that the water had gradually become cleaner, although by no means had all the factories been destroyed. This example proves that solutions do exist to limit pollution without bringing industry to a halt. Of course, I am no expert in this field, and it is up to the specialists to find such solutions.

Has the time come to adopt an agricultural policy more in keeping with the specific customs of developing countries, one which would attempt to sustain and encourage the preservation of traditional eating habits, rather than try to impose Western views on agricultural practices?

It is important in such cases to adapt to the specific circumstances and conditions of each place. The use of chemical products like fertilizers or insecticides is undoubtedly a temporary necessity in order to increase productivity and prevent the destruction of crops. It does, however, have a very negative aspect, which is pollution. In certain countries it might be necessary to intervene where there is a risk of famine or other difficulties confronting the population. These difficulties are quite often due to the fact that the budget is given over to the military rather than to agriculture. On the other hand, in places where, due to natural causes such as droughts or infertile soil, the population suffers from a lack of edible resources, it is imperative to try whatever means available to increase the productivity of the soil. In other cases, where circumstances allow, it is certainly preferable to maintain a more traditional form of agriculture, where nature and its preservation are shown greater respect.

TO SERVE HUMANITY

Your Holiness, you were an exceptional child. Children who are concerned about the future of the planet have formed an association. What is your message to them?

The future is what lies ahead of us and consequently it is extremely important. Children bear the responsibility for this future. Given the fact that human nature is basically good, children, when they are still very young, do not really differentiate one person from another. Their love, their good-heartedness, are spontaneous. For example, they attach more importance to the smile of the person in front of them than to their race, nationality, or culture. I greatly appreciate the value of such an attitude, and it gives me great hope for the future.

In other respects, however, I am quite concerned. Children are naturally warm-hearted and kind, but certain aspects of the education they receive increase the divisions among them, and this has the effect of creating a gap between one child and others. It seems very important, therefore, that along with education this basic kindness, found in its natural state in children, must be fostered. By this I mean that education should be in harmony with the child's essentially kind nature. The most important element is that children be raised in a climate of love and tenderness. Although from an ideal perspective human qualities ought to be developed in conjunction with kindness, I often say that if I had to choose between important general qualities and kindness, I believe I would choose kindness.

Intelligence and the education with which human beings are endowed, however important they might be, are not enough to build the future. Our mind must be filled with altruism, by experiencing basic human values such as love for one's neighbor. We must be permeated with kindness, our state of mind must be positive. Let us enrich our intelligence with these qualities and put to good use what education can give us, in order that together with the society in which we live we may find fulfillment and happiness.

Why do children and parents in the West have such difficulty in getting along?

I really don't know. There are so many factors and conditions contributing to family conflicts, such as habits and customs, and the example we set for children. It is of course very sad to witness the disappearance of love between parents and children. I do not think it is possible to isolate one common factor responsible for so much conflict. The causes are many, and when we try to resolve the problems, we must view them in their entirety.

The political and economic views of Western countries seemed to work quite well during the Sixties, but this is no longer the case in the Nineties. People are no longer content. How can the situation be improved?

From early childhood on I have been very interested in technology. Some people maintain that development per se is not entirely desirable; in my opinion, this is not the case. I think it all depends on our attitude. Technology is an instrument, it does what we ask it to do, and we have the power to use it for good or for evil. Everything depends therefore upon our motivation and the manner in which we are going to use it. I think we are witnessing in our time a tremendous expansion of knowledge, but people's interest in the development of kindness, good-heartedness, and altruistic love is perhaps not quite as obvious as their interest in knowledge.

Having said that, I do think that things are now becoming very clear. Human beings are not the product of a machine, and cannot therefore aspire to true happiness by depending solely on external circumstances. We do indeed need a minimum of worldly prosperity, but that is not the source of happiness. We must seek the true causes of happiness and satisfaction in ourselves. They must be developed inside us. I think this point is very clear.

Although it is difficult to explain, I am going to try to express what I mean by this affirmation. First of all, we must recognize that happiness is to be found in our mind. Those who think solely in terms of science and technology, maintaining that everything can be resolved and achieved with material progress, have an extreme point of view. I think we must acknowledge the limits of such an approach. If we start by locating these limits we will not feel so shocked when we encounter external obstacles.

I think that when we are faced with difficulties, it is preferable not to examine them too closely. Instead, let us step back and consider them with a more open mind, let us look at the bigger picture. In this way the solution will come to us more easily. For example, when confronted with very serious problems, if we try to deal with them without taking any distance from them, they will seem unbearable, and we will see nothing but the negative aspects. If, on the other hand, we observe them with a certain distance and approach them with a much more open attitude, examining the problem from different angles, this will help us see the positive aspects of the situation.

I think it is vital to combine the natural intelligence we all possess with courage, so that we may develop true self-confidence. My own experience has taught me that this attitude is very conducive to inner peace.

What measures could politicians take to make the population happier?

I think this role is not limited strictly to politicians. It concerns everybody—teachers, scientists, political theorists, psychologists, all those who work with sciences of the mind, intellectuals—in short, everyone should be searching for means to bring about inner peace. Medical science is discovering more and more connections between mental serenity and physical health. Such research deserves to be taken further.

I must say that the media has at present a very important role to play. Our media belong to a modern age and, as such, I believe they act in a way as teachers, to stimulate people's minds. Journalists play a very particular role.

I would like to express a few opinions on this matter. I have the impression that the mass media pay far too much attention to the

negative aspects of human activity, and this gives the general public
the impression that human nature as a whole is negative. When you
have such an impression you automatically become discouraged, and
the danger of losing hope is quite real. Humanity suffers from so
many problems, even if it is only one family's. Despite the innumerable difficulties encountered by human beings, the possibility for
transformation does exist—we can improve our situation, because
sympathy and compassion are part of our nature. If we associate our
human intelligence with a motivation of kindness, we have the possibility of changing our lives, of transforming society. I consider this
to be an essential point.

That is why I think that when your subject matter deals with
human beings, it would be better if there were more of a balance. Of
course, all the negative aspects of human life are not without importance, and they provide good copy for newspapers. But at the same
time, do not neglect to show the positive aspects of life that are based
in human nature and intelligence.

There has been some discussion recently in certain countries about
the role of the mass media. Must everything be reported? How should
it be reported? What part of private life should remain inaccessible
to the media? I have a few ideas on the subject, particularly where
leaders are concerned. From time to time some public figures might
abuse their position, showing neither moral principles nor self-discipline. In such cases, I think the media alone have the power to verify and expose such behavior; that is why I support them in their
activity and I appreciate this inquisitive aspect of journalists, poking
their noses everywhere.

There should be no discrepancy between the external appearance
and the inner life of an honest person. I think the media should show
the public that certain renowned personalities hide a very different
aspect behind a pleasant facade. In such instances I do rather favor
this type of interference in people's private lives, but we must not forget, however, that our fundamental common goal is to serve humanity in order to improve society. Do not act in error, on the impulse
of negative motives. I think that if we did not expose all the evils of

society, such as drugs, murder, sexual abuse, and exploitation of children, innocent people would still continue to suffer from them daily. If you explain things clearly, the public will eventually pay attention and find means to reduce the suffering they cause.

I also think that when people speak about morals or ethics they often associate these qualities with religious concepts. I think it is very important to dissociate these two notions: morality and religion. Religion helps, of course, to strengthen morality, to sustain it and develop it, but when one speaks of altruism and brotherly love, for example, one must realize that this morality exists by and of itself, independent of religion, because it is founded upon the basic nature of human beings—kindness and love.

What is your view on birth control and what do you think of abortion?

I generally respond to this question by explaining the Buddhist point of view, which considers all forms of life, even insects, to be inestimably precious—particularly human life. If you look at it this way, all forms of birth control should be proscribed. However, because the number of precious human lives is now considerable, we are seriously urging people to consider birth control, as it is the only means of limiting demographic growth. As I have already pointed out, given the depletion of the earth's resources I am in favor of a nonviolent form of birth control.

Abortion is defined as an act of killing. The Vinaya tradition states as a cardinal rule that no human being whosoever must be killed, and this includes the fetus. There are, however, exceptional cases which are a source of intense suffering for certain members of a family and which must be taken into consideration, like that of a pregnant mother whose life is at risk during childbirth or who would give birth to a severely handicapped child.

How can we help those in great physical suffering, for whom following the path of enlightenment seems impossible, beyond their strength?

There are several types of physical illness. Those which seriously affect the patient's mind are immeasurably pitiful and tragic; but other painful physical ordeals, like chronic illness, paralysis, or other serious conditions, leave the mind alert and allow for a certain level of spiritual involvement. The study of the Dharma is not a physical act; it concerns the use of the mind and an inner attitude. Sufferers can be introduced to meditations devoted, for example, to love, courage, faith, and compassion; such meditations will give them confidence and confer meaning and dignity to their lives. But this introduction must be done very skillfully.

Personally, I think that such patients can engage in profound and intense study. If they profess no particular faith, we must remain attentive to their preferences and their spiritual needs. To impose views or practices on someone which go against their temperament and inner inclinations would be absurd. Choose with care the moment for speaking, and make certain of the receptivity of the one listening to you. The essence of your help must be to preserve an atmosphere of peace so that the person's mind will remain calm and relaxed. This is a crucial point.

What can be done when one realizes one has AIDS or a similar incurable disease?

Once again, how one reacts to this type of illness will depend upon one's spiritual involvement. I do not know what to say to atheists or to those who have no particular religious beliefs. But I would like to say that whatever a person's capacity for reflection, society must neither abandon nor marginalize that person, for this would reduce the sufferer to feeling rejected and helpless, without protection. One must make sure that the sick person never feels excluded. This is where society has a great responsibility.

If a person has no hope left of living—someone in a deep coma, for example—is it important to keep them alive artificially? What is the karma of taking life in order to prevent further suffering?

We have to look at the problem from the point of view of the ill person. Is the mind still awake, alert, capable of thinking and reasoning? If yes, it is of capital importance to let that person live, even just one more day, for he or she still has the possibility of developing virtuous states of mind, such as compassion and altruism. If they have sunk into a deep coma, where the mind cannot function in any case, we must then take into consideration, among other things, the desires of the family and decide who will be responsible for euthanasia. It is a delicate problem, one that cannot be answered on the basis of general suggestions.

Above all, one must consider the motivation behind the act. Buddhism instructs us not to take the life of any living being. If a person suffers, he must assume this difficult condition and purify it. But it would be a mistake to remain indifferent to their suffering simply by saying it is their karma and there is nothing to be done. Every one of us has accumulated his or her own karma. It has already been acquired; its potential is within us. The future is therefore already in our hands. As our difficulties, illnesses, infirmities, and so on are the fruit of earlier negative actions we have committed, it is difficult to escape. Threatened with sickness and suffering we try all the means at our disposal to ward them off, to relieve our difficulties; and even when we realize we are powerless to cure or to comfort, we must remember that all these problems are the result of our own past actions.

How, then, can we help someone in a coma?

If the person is a believer, help him within the context of the religion he practices. I am not certain how precise an answer can be given. From the Buddhist point of view, one should have been prepared before such a tragic event, for once you are in a coma it is a bit late to be thinking of spiritual practices.

How can one stop being an alcoholic?

The best thing is to seek advice from doctors. Leaving aside any consideration about the religious beliefs of the person in question, the easiest thing is to reflect on the obvious detriments of excessive consumption of alcohol, and to realize how much alcoholism destroys both mind and body, to understand the way in which alcohol isolates you from others and marginalizes you, and so on. A clear vision of all these drawbacks and the development of a strong determination and desire to stop drinking will, I am certain, allow you to change. But if you are unable to reflect upon this in a constructive manner, it would be preferable to undergo one of the numerous medical treatments available at present.

If a Tibetan kills a yak in order to feed his family, is this a negative act? Or a bodyguard kills someone in order to protect your life? How are we to interpret examples like these?

Of course these are negative acts. The karmic impact of each act depends upon a number of factors, such as the intention which motivates the act, the act itself, and the thoughts which follow.

What are improper sexual attitudes? What do you think of homosexuality, for example?

Something may be considered improper in terms of organs, time, and place—when sexual relations involve inappropriate parts of the body, or when they occur at an unsuitable time or place. These are the terms Buddhists use to describe sexual misconduct. The inappropriate parts of the body are the mouth and the anus, and sexual intercourse involving those parts of the body, whether with a man or a woman, is considered sexual misconduct. Masturbation as well.

As for when sexual intercourse takes place, if it is during the day it is also held to be a form of misconduct, as is having intercourse with a partner who professes to certain principles such as sexual abstinence or celibacy, even if those vows are only temporary. To force someone to have intercourse also comes under the category of improper time.

Inappropriate locations include temples, places of devotion, or positions where one of the partners is uncomfortable. A sexual act is deemed proper when the couple uses the organs created for sexual intercourse and nothing else. To have sexual relations with a prostitute paid by you and not by a third person does not, on the other hand, constitute improper behavior. All these examples define what is and what is not proper sexual behavior according to Buddhist morality.

Homosexuality, whether it is between men or between women, is not improper in itself. What is improper is the use of organs already defined as inappropriate for sexual contact. Is this clear?

How does Buddhism explain the consciousness of tiny beings such as insects or bacteria? Do all animate beings have consciousness? Might one also then speak of consciousness in trees, plants, stones, all those things which seem to us inanimate? Do trees have Buddhanature?

I have talked about this with scientists. We managed to agree, more or less, on the fact that consciousness, the mind, accompanies everything which moves, by which we mean the ability to move by oneself—a faculty which trees do not possess. Of course, roots move as they grow, but they do not have their own mobility other than that of their growth. So we cannot call a tree a "sentient being," that is, endowed with a mind. But we concluded that the tiniest cell, like the amoeba, could be considered a sentient creature because it has the ability to move by itself.

As we cannot qualify vegetable growth, such as grass, as sentient, we do not consider it to have Buddhanature. As for carnivorous plants, I am not qualified to judge whether the act of trapping their prey is the result of a purely chemical interaction or whether they possess a consciousness. The question remains open to debate. However, in some cases, one can raise the question. This flower, for example: is it an inanimate vegetable—without consciousness—or a sentient being? We are sometimes allowed to doubt because certain Buddhist texts refer to sentient beings which may appear in the form of inanimate objects, or plants, and so on. For this reason, one cannot say for certain whether a flower is sentient or not, because we do not know if a sentient being has manifested as it.

Buddhism insists greatly upon the protection of nature, trees, plants—not that these plant varieties are animate beings, and therefore creatures worthy of compassion, but because it is nature itself which allows many living creatures to survive and which protects them. If a town is burned to the ground, are not the homes of a great many people destroyed? The destruction of nature is no different, because a great numbers of animals lose their source of food, shelter, and survival.

As for microscopic animals, according to Buddhist texts our body is known to contain a considerable number. One figure mentions more than 80,000, which signifies a very great number. From what dimension, at what stage of their evolution, can these infinitesimal creatures be considered sentient beings? There is nothing I can add except to say that however tiny an animal may be, if we speak of it as an animal then it must have some form of animate life, and, consequently of consciousness.

Can you tell us about the notion of collective karma, the karma of a nation such as Cambodia or Tibet? What does this collective karma represent?

It is conceivable to speak of the collective karma of a nation. However, although the cumulative effects of karma may be experienced simultaneously by one and the same group of people, it does not necessarily follow that all their karma was created at the same time. I don't believe it is necessary for the causes of a collective karma to have been created all at the same time; they are produced individually at different times. The strength of these acts in conjunction with numerous other factors may result in a collective karma, which is then experienced by a group of people or an entire nation.

There are war criminals in many European countries, in Eastern Europe, and in other countries in Asia, such as Cambodia and Vietnam, who have never been tried, or have even in some cases received amnesty before being brought to trial. What do you think of this?

It is disgraceful to see that many countries recently liberated from oppressive regimes have turned to resentment and a desire for vengeance when they should, instead, be forgiving and accepting. This is not a time for vengeance and settling accounts in newly democratic countries. On the contrary, the time has come to rebuild both nation and society. I have already expressed my feelings about this in my visits to some of these countries. In China, the political regime remains oppressive despite a certain economic liberalization. Human rights are constantly violated throughout the country and more particularly in the regions considered minority regions, significantly in Tibet, which is in fact an occupied country.

I greatly appreciate and admire the very noble actions of organizations such as Amnesty International that work with great sincerity, efficiency, and energy in the domain of human rights violations.

You speak of the inner disarmament which must accompany external disarmament. I would like you to be more specific about what this inner disarmament means when you are face-to-face with the enemy, when hatred stands before you. In the book The Ways of the Heart, *you evoke the possibility of creating an army of international troops in the future. How would this work, given the fact that you advocate nonviolence? Would these troops be armed?*

Everyone knows very well that the potential for killing will exist for as long as weapons are brandished between countries, or even simply within one country. In any case, something must be done about the trafficking of arms because the situation has become both terrifying and irresponsible. We have been thinking very seriously about the problem of arms and armament: close examination reveals that the military institution is the primary cause of the destructive situation and that reigns of terror are imposed by weapons. Therefore, there will always be a risk of open conflict for as long as military institutions exist, on one side as on the other.

This is why demilitarization has become essential, on a gradual basis, of course. You begin with denuclearization, then you abolish chemical and biological weapons, and finally you abandon conventional weaponry. There must be first of all an international guarantee overseeing the process, which would also control arms sales—a domain where you find certain unscrupulous individuals. In order to supervise this disarmament, there could be a relatively insignificant law enforcement body, a kind of international police. The United Nations are already quite involved in military actions of liberation; we could have a regional or international force to keep watch on a totally disarmed country. My main idea is that these collective forces would act like peacekeeping forces. In that way everyone might eventually become a bodhisattva, and that requires no weapons at all! But I think it will be difficult.

Some people might not know what is meant by inner disarmament. I think that hatred is our worst enemy. It is the enemy of inner peace, friendship, and harmony, three key factors for positive development, for the creation of a better world. Hatred must be reduced, and compassion and sympathy developed. This is what I call inner disarmament.

How do you define humanity?

This question deals, of course, with the reality of the world of phenomena, which has several levels. At the highest level, we cannot find an absolute existence for that which we call reality.

Now on a more general basis, I often say that the true essence of humankind is kindness. There are other qualities which come from education or knowledge, but it is essential, if one wishes to be a genuine human being and impart satisfying meaning to one's existence, to have a good heart.

What exactly is the happiness connected with the Dharma? Is it a sensation?

Happiness is of two varieties: a happiness which is a pleasant sensation, an agreeable experience; and another that is much more profound in the satisfaction it gives. When you think of the Dharma and put it into practice, you are said to be accumulating merits, virtues, because all the kinds of happiness and satisfaction are the direct or indirect consequence of positive, virtuous acts. Need I reaffirm that an authentic spiritual commitment is the shortest path to peace and serenity? Peace of mind, mental tranquility, may not necessarily be felt as a specific sensation, but can provoke a physical sensation of joy and happiness. The peace and bliss of *nirvana* do not constitute an actual state belonging to the realm of sensation, but rather a state of complete liberation from suffering and the ties which chain us to the cycle of uncontrolled rebirth. From this point of view, it is a state of permanent happiness. Buddhahood is described in terms of total bliss, absolute beatitude. If you wish to take the question one step further and ask: what is the nature of this bliss?, we are forced to reply, of course, that it is inconceivable, unimaginable, totally beyond the reach of our intellectual capacities.

How can mental courage be developed? Isn't it a positive attribute?

Without doubt, courage is a positive and necessary attitude. If you lack courage, try to tell yourself continually, "I will be brave, I will be brave," and persist in this line of thinking.

How can courage be developed? First of all, you have to be able to identify each emotion and isolate those which, at the slightest incident, provoke and trouble your mind. You know this type of negative emotion, brought on by little events of no importance—without reason, without rational motivation, your mind reacts in confusion and agitation. Another category of factors, which includes compassion, love, and kindness, has at its base healthy and positive premises. If you think of them you will increase your courage and your moral strength; and when you meditate seriously on the fundamentally unsatisfactory nature of cyclic existence, a profound feeling of revulsion will arise in you, creating an urgent need to free yourself from it.

This powerful drive, the specific goal of which is liberation from samsara, is something I would qualify—without being able to ascertain it 100 percent—as a positive state of mind, because it stems from a healthy thought process and reasons verified by experience. As we can classify the practices of the Mahayana into two categories—method, also known as skillful means, and wisdom—I think we can assimilate these qualities to method and intelligence to wisdom. It is certain that method corresponds to the positive aspects of our reactions, and wisdom to the display of our intelligence.

How to develop courage—this is a daunting question! In fact I believe I can affirm that the entirety of Shantideva's *Bodhicharyavatara,* from the beginning of the first chapter to the end of the tenth and final, has as its theme the way to awaken and cultivate courage and determination. However, according to the disposition, mentality, and intelligence of different individuals, some might prefer the validity of one technique suggested by the text, and others might be attracted by the way another works.

I greatly appreciate the words of Geshe Potawa: "Samsara has neither beginning nor source and cannot therefore end on its own. It is not comparable to the fruit of a tree which, if one does not tend it, will grow bigger, ripen, and finally fall from the branch once it is rotten." If you find it depressing to live in cyclic existence and it is therefore imperative to break out of it, it will do you no good whatsoever to simply wait for freedom to come. Time alone cannot bring cyclic existence to its end. You must take the initiative; you must consciously take the first step to deliberately reverse the process of samsara. To sit there and do nothing but wait for cyclic existence to cease on its own is evidence of pointless, wasted hope.

What is the difference between non-attachment and indifference?

There is a great difference. Indifference implies complete disinterest toward the object in question, whereas non-attachment carries a certain implication.

To clarify, let us see what attachment is. There are two types: the first is induced by a state of mind disturbed by craving or by other negative mental factors, and must be abandoned. The second is the attraction for objects of compassion—where attraction does not result from negative thoughts or emotions—which must be deepened and strengthened.

When we meditate on emptiness, we are moved to relinquish our erroneous understanding of phenomena and events, for it is a false understanding that leads us to believe that things have a solid, independent existence. It is vital to correct this faulty understanding, but this in no way prevents us from maintaining our consciousness to be capable at all times of discriminating between that which must be cultivated and that which must be abandoned, and from trying to increase the potential of healthy, positive qualities, ridding ourselves all the while of negative and harmful tendencies. Our discriminating faculties remain intact.

In the same vein, the bodhisattva must uproot and completely eliminate arrogance and self-conceit. The bodhisattva's humility must place him or her quite naturally below all other creatures. But that in no way hinders the extraordinary confidence and remarkable courage manifest in their commitment to free all beings from suffering. This example of great compassion, free from any form of negative attachment, proves that such behavior attaches greater importance to the well-being of others than to one's personal happiness.

It is by using one's intelligence and by undertaking spiritual practices where both method and creative mental faculties are necessary that one will learn to see the subtle nuances between that which feeds the ego, a function of attachment, and the positive qualities dedicated to the good of others. Only the union between method and wisdom can lead to the development of valid faculties of discernment. I generally say that to speak of the ego necessarily implies speaking of strong self-awareness. One of the forms of the ego cares little about others and does not concern itself with their happiness, even going so far as to exploit for its own benefit whatever makes them happy! This mental attitude, obviously very negative, must be fought.

On the other hand, another aspect of the ego might be displayed in great self-confidence, the kind of confidence which enables us to say: "I can do this or that. I am capable of working for the good of everyone. I will attain perfect enlightenment for the salvation of all beings." This feeling should not be eliminated. On the contrary, it should be developed and strengthened. As you progress along the path, the mind remains relaxed and calm on the surface, yet all the while profoundly alert and vigilant, displaying with wisdom introspection and attention.

What is the difference between anger and hatred?

I personally make a distinction between these two disturbances of the mind. Hatred is linked to spite against someone and can never be motivated by compassion. It must therefore be completely eliminated. Anger, on the other hand is the fruit of an immediate emotional reaction which, in the tantric context, can be used on the spiritual path. Anger may on occasion also be the expression of compassion, for example, in order to serve as a catalyst or impulse for urgent action.

Could you define the notion of having an enemy?

When you "see red" from anger toward someone, ask your choleric state of mind what an enemy is. The chapter devoted to tolerance and patience in the *Bodhicharyavatara* by Shantideva defines the enemy as someone who threatens our lives or our friends, our belongings or their possessions, and so on. The friend of our enemies is also considered an enemy. The aspect of the practice of the transformation of thought (Tibetan: *lodjong*), where one establishes equality between oneself and others, introduces the idea that there are no longer any enemies or friends. Not that their existence is denied: enemies exist; friends do, too. This practice suggests rather that there is no longer any reason to be angry with those we consider our enemies, or to become more attached in any particular way with certain people because they are our friends or relatives. Seen from a certain angle, so-and-so is my enemy because he harms me, but from another angle I can see him as a friend, since he gives me the opportunity to practice patience and develop tolerance. This point of view sees him not as inimical, but as useful and helpful.

Taking into account Buddhist teachings, how can we understand the experience of violent events such as war?

The most important thing is to avoid killing. The thought that one might be allowed to take a human life must be completely banished from one's mind.

PART II

SPIRITUALITY
AND POLITICS

COMPASSION

On behalf of all the people of Tibet, I would like to thank all those who have taken an interest in the culture of Tibet and its traditions, both spiritual and secular. I thank you for all you are doing to make sure these traditions do not disappear.

I am going to speak today of peace of mind. The reason Tibetan culture is so important—at least, it seems to me—is that our culture has great potential for promoting peace of mind. During the extremely difficult period we have known recently in Tibet, one of the factors which has helped us to remain determined and not lose hope is this aspect of our own culture.

Our civilization is such that it has allowed us to preserve our serenity and our inner peace in spite of all the trials and difficult situations we have known. Recently I have had more and more contact with Western scientists, and we have been speaking about the frustration experienced by human beings and of various possible remedies for that frustration. The scientists questioned me at length about the mental health and state of mind of Tibetan people, and they were very surprised to discover that despite all the trauma the Tibetans have experienced, they manage to preserve a stable mental state. This has been observed in particular among those who spent long years in Chinese prisons and labor camps.

I would like to share with you an example. The associate abbot of the Namgyal monastery, who was recently exiled to India, was imprisoned in 1959, then sent to a Chinese labor camp—he was incarcerated a total of eighteen years. After he reached his monastery in exile, we had a chat together. He told me of his life and his experiences. He mentioned that while he was in the hands of the Chinese, he was in great danger for the following reason: he explained that he almost lost the compassion he felt for his torturers. I found this remarkable!

I often tease this man, telling him that despite all those difficult years spent at the mercy of the Chinese, his face has hardly changed. Although he is older than me, I believe he has even less white hair than I do—you probably can't see mine today, I shaved my head this morning! Above all, he has kept his wonderful smile. All this is possible, or so it seems to me, because of Tibetan and Buddhist culture.

Perhaps my modest experience might serve as an example. As a Buddhist monk, I have been trained in the practice, the philosophy, and the teachings of Buddhism, but not at all with the view of having to cope with the demands of modern life. I have had to handle enormous responsibilities. I lost my freedom at the age of sixteen, and my country when I was twenty-four. For thirty-four years I have lived in exile, a refugee in a foreign country. All this time, while we have been working for the exiled Tibetan community, our country has known immeasurable destruction and suffering. Despite all this tragedy I find that as far as my mind, peace, and serenity are concerned, I am not doing too badly.

On occasion tourists come back from Tibet or from the refugee camps in India with the false impression that Tibetans can't have suffered all that much because they seem very happy and are always smiling. This misconception is the only disadvantage of our mental attitude.

How can we develop inner peace and serenity in our mind? I think human nature is basically good. It is true that we are also made up of jealousy and hatred, but nevertheless I believe our dominant characteristics are affection and kindness. From the first day of our lives until our last breath, the very foundation of our existence is affection and human warmth. It is a well-known fact that children raised in an affectionate family have greater success in developing their human qualities, while those who grow up in the absence of the favorable conditions of love and compassion end up with a far more negative behavior in life and create tension wherever they go. The absence or the presence of compassion and love in a family therefore has a very obvious effect. According to doctors and scientists, a calm mental state is a critical factor in a person's health. In addition, from the first weeks of life, physical contact, whether with the mother or someone else, is of prime importance for the awakening and development of the child's brain.

We all know that on days when we are in a good mood, when the whole world seems to be smiling at us, we can accept predicaments or bad news more easily than if our mind is already upset, frustrated, or troubled, when the slightest incident might cause us to explode with negative emotions. If we make a habit of being governed by these negative emotions, we will lose our appetite, sleep badly, perhaps become ill, and lose a few years of our life itself as a result. So mental calmness is very important.

I think that in the West people are very precise and are more interested in action than in motivation. For me, motivation is more important, for it is sometimes difficult to judge the value of an act without referring, precisely, to what lies behind it. After all, the energy of life, of human activity, is intention. This takes place in our thoughts, and just as there exist in the outside world countless varied substances— some beneficial, others harmful—which we try either to accumulate or avoid, respectively, there also exist in the inner world, in the mind, thousands and thousands of thoughts of all kinds. Some are very useful because they make us happy and give us inner tranquility and strength. Others disturb us, leaving us demoralized or depressed, sometimes even pushing us toward suicide.

Thoughts and emotions are therefore either positive or negative. We must first of all establish their worth before we try to encourage the positive ones and eliminate the others. In this way, we can cultivate inner peace. An ability to distinguish beneficial thoughts from those which are not makes all the difference. As a rule, we do not take our thoughts and our emotions into account. We simply consider them to be an integral part of ourselves, and believe that there is nothing we can do about them. When we must deal with a problem or danger, anger and hatred seem to protect us and give us renewed energy. However, attachment creeps insidiously into our minds; we treat it like a comfortable old friend. But in the end this "old friend" will lead us down the garden path. Some of these emotions, like anger or fear, reveal their true face almost immediately. Other emotions, like attachment, make their negative effects felt over time. Once we recognize the characteristics of negative attitudes and correctly identify their consequences, we will know how to be more wary of them.

From then on we can begin to detach from them and cultivate the opposite attitude—compassion, forgiveness, and sympathy. In this way we can progressively strengthen positive emotions as we weaken our negative emotions. Even if they do continue to appear, they will be passing emotions and not leave too visible a mark upon our mind. In some cases, it is better to express anger or resentment provoked by past events in order to rid ourselves of these feelings. But, in general, if we let anger or other negative emotions flow freely, we will get used to them and eventually lose our temper more and more frequently. That is why I think it is very useful to impose a certain discipline in shaping one's mind. Discipline is not imposed from the outside; it is our own intelligence that must impose it from within. In this way we accept it fully.

In training the mind, time is of crucial importance. We must not expect to be completely transformed in a few minutes or even a few weeks, by thinking, for example, that because we have received the blessing of an enlightened individual we will be able to obtain immediate results. Such an attitude is hardly realistic. It takes time, sometimes years, perhaps even decades. But if we persevere, keeping our goal and the means to attain it in sight, we will certainly progress over time.

How can we lessen anger and hatred? In some cases, if it is motivated by compassion, for example, anger can be a positive thing. Hatred, on the other hand, is always negative. We must measure and understand the harmful nature of distressing feelings such as hatred. As I have already said, hatred makes us lose our health and our friends, and it will eventually spoil our entire life. Negative emotions create problems on all levels—individual, family, community, national, even international. The history of humanity has shown that those who have inflicted unspeakable suffering on others were driven by boundless hatred and greed. At times such behavior was simply through ignorance. This does not mean that these people are bad at heart— they are human beings, after all. But they allowed their minds to be dominated and confused by negative emotions which eventually turned them into murderers.

Again, if we look at the history of humanity, we will find that the great majority of successful endeavors were accomplished by people who were altruistic and at peace with themselves. The majority of great musicians and artists possess this inner peace. There are exceptions, of course, but it generally holds true that artistic creation springs from an inner tranquility that is conducive for the expression of one's deepest feelings. In this way, artists create happiness and bring inspiration to others.

We can also take the contemporary example of Mahatma Gandhi, an extraordinary human being who had great self-discipline. He needed very little to be content. Despite his Western education and his awareness of the benefits to be had from that civilization in terms of material comfort or opportunity, he chose to live in India in great simplicity, almost like a beggar. This reflects his self-discipline and altruism. Everything positive that human beings have managed to accomplish has been, in my opinion, a result of these positive emotions of the mind.

My own experience, as well as that of others, has shown me the degree to which positive mental attitudes bring happiness to oneself and to others, and to what degree negative attitudes can be destructive. On that basis it is up to each individual to make every possible effort to develop his or her mind.

Human beings live in society. Even though it is more agreeable to have lots of friends and no enemies, everyone finds both friends and enemies among other people. Friends and enemies do not exist as such. Friendship and enmity result from different factors, of which the primary one is our own mental attitude. When we are open to others and ready to offer them our friendship and affection, this immediately creates a good environment. Without even realizing it, other people come up to us with a smile on their face—not a tense, artificial smile, but a sincere one. But if we feed on bad intentions and negative thoughts, if we do not take into account the rights and wishes of others; in short, if we think only of ourselves and have a tendency to exploit others for our own ends, the situation will suffer. Even close family members will stay away in the end. Thus it becomes clear that friends and enemies are the product of our own personal attitude.

Some think, mistakenly, that money creates friends. Nothing could be less certain—it also creates enemies! Let us think for a moment of those who greet us with a big smile on their face: are they our friends or the friends of our money? There's no telling. For as long as we have money, they will certainly come and share a bottle of champagne, and everything will be fine. But when the money is no longer there, friends begin to disappear, as if by magic. It becomes impossible to reach them on the phone, or their response is abrupt. Money and material goods are of course necessary, but they are not the essential thing. True wealth is to be found within.

Compassion, forgiveness, hope, and perseverance are positive attitudes which all great religions try to develop and strengthen. You need not necessarily be a believer—every person has the right to accept or refuse religion—in order to amplify these positive attitudes of the mind. We should remember that the great world religions carry the same message and encourage the same human qualities. Although religious dogma may differ, the central message remains the same. On the basis of this common ground, the message of love and compassion will spread to the far corners of the world if all those who follow a spiritual path work together in harmony and mutual respect.

But if those who advocate these same human qualities quarrel with and criticize one another, how will they be able to communicate this message to others? People will surely say, not without a certain irony, "Look at them! Where are tolerance and mutual respect? They can't even get along." If we want to help humanity in a practical way, we must to begin by setting an example of mutual respect, harmony, and togetherness in the eyes of the world. Seen from a distance, differences can seem enormous. But if we approach others and share their experiences, we will better understand how to get along despite doctrinal differences, and how to develop together the positive aspects of human existence. It is therefore of the utmost importance to maintain good relations, and for different religious movements to communicate with each other. Despite all the conflicts caused by religious discord, whether in Bosnia or Africa, there have been encouraging steps towards reconciliation. But a sustained effort must be made in this direction!

I recently saw a documentary about the suffering of Tibet, which included the testimony of a monk who had been incarcerated for more than thirty-three years—twenty-four in prison and nine in labor camps. He had suffered the most awful torture imaginable, which left him handicapped for life. How can we conceive of peace of mind, which implies serenity and virtue, when we hear a story like this? Wouldn't anger and pragmatism be a more appropriate response?

The most important thing is to not be indifferent, to feel strongly about the situation but in a constructive way, if you see what I mean. We must not be overwhelmed by our feelings to the point of paralysis. I'm not sure if I've understood what you are asking, but if the idea is to maintain inner calm effectively when confronted with situations like the one you have described, then it depends in large part upon each individual's own level of spiritual development.

Considering the terrible ordeals you and your people have known and continue to endure, do you have any thoughts about nature, about gardens? Do you consider them to be one of the more obvious symbols of civilization? What message can a landscape offer, in your opinion? Can gardens and landscapes help us to find peace of mind, to identify and adopt the path to wisdom?

I do indeed believe that, particularly when our spirit is troubled, if we go outside and look at the land around us, breathe in the fresh air and listen to the birds singing, we can find a temporary peace of mind. After all, in spite of all our knowledge and abilities, we are still part of nature, we are its product. Thousands of years ago our ancestors lived much closer to nature. Today we still have traces of that life in us: even in the most modern homes we like to have wooden furniture and green plants—it's in our blood.

In the past all of life was based on trees. Their flowers gave us decoration, their fruit gave us nourishment, their leaves and fibers clothed us and provided us with shelter. We took refuge in their branches for protection from wild animals. We used wood for heat, and for canes to bear our weight when we grew old, and to make weapons to defend ourselves. We were very close to trees. Today, surrounded by sophisticated machinery and high-performance computers in our ultramodern offices, it is easy to forget our ties with nature. It is normal to try and improve the quality of our lives through science and technology. But at the same time it is important to know the limitations of such progress and to remain aware of the fact that we still depend on nature. If the environment were to be radically altered there would be nothing we could do to protect ourselves. That is why all our thoughts and acts must follow the Middle Way.

In our Western minds there is often confusion between repression and the search for inner peace. When we repress something, we take everything that is a problem in our lives and hide it away in a little corner of ourselves, thinking that we will be able to forget it and go on living without having to deal with it. What do you think of this art of repression?

I think I already touched briefly on this problem by saying that in some cases, that of fear in particular, it is not necessarily a bad thing to express your emotions in order to be rid of them. But I do think this presents a certain danger. Indeed, if we lack inner discipline and we let all the emotions that go through our heads come out, on the pretext that they must be expressed, we will reach a point of considerable excess and may even have difficulty in respecting the laws of our country. Socially or individually, we do need a certain inner discipline in order to direct our thoughts in a constructive way. Human emotions have no limits, and the strength of negative emotions is infinite.

But I do not think that we can talk about repression in that case. On the contrary, this is something quite positive. We study and practice in order to eliminate our ignorance in stages. Practice can often seem difficult. When we are tired we might not feel like carrying on. But nevertheless, as we become aware of the benefits of practice we will impose a certain discipline and go on with our effort. In studying we expand our knowledge, but that does not mean that we repress our ignorance!

ETHICS AND SOCIETY

A set of ethics is as crucial for a politician as it is for one who practices a religion.

—*His Holiness the Dalai Lama*

Today we are going to talk about ethics in society; that is, what constitutes righteous, honest conduct. We can distinguish two sets of ethics on which I will comment: one is linked to religion, to spirituality, and the other is not. A certain type of morality, of fair and honest behavior, is necessarily linked to inner spirituality, but as a rule I believe in the authenticity of a set of ethics implemented for our own good and for others.

We can say that an act is immoral or improper to the extent that it causes harm to others. We must also distinguish the immediate or temporary effects of an act from its ultimate effects, its long-term consequences. For although an act may be profitable at the time, it can turn into something negative in the long run. Other acts which may seem quite difficult initially will yield totally positive results over a longer period of time. Whatever the case, it is the ultimate outcome that matters.

We will speak, therefore, of ethics or morality—even where animals are concerned—from this point of view; in other words, on how they are beneficial to others. Some animals who live in groups show signs of altruistic behavior, limited of course, but altruistic all the same, with regard to those around them. We can observe among animals—who have neither laws, religion, nor a constitution—acts which might be qualified as good or bad. If there is morality among animals, all the more reason for it to exist among humans, whether or not they consider themselves religious.

It is principally the intention behind an act that determines whether it is positive or negative, beneficial or harmful. An act perceived as somewhat abrupt or forceful may still be right, if its motivation is deep and admirable, and if it brings good to others. On the other hand, sometimes an extremely evil intention or purpose may be hidden under cover of a seemingly very gentle act. I believe an act to be good if it is motivated by altruism, the desire to do good for others, whereas an act is said to be negative when it is prompted by malice, the desire to harm others. In this way, we can define the outline of a set of ethics which need not be based in religious concepts or beliefs. Moreover, animals are very aware of our behavior: if we go up to a dog with hidden intentions, for example, the dog will know and sense it. But if we approach him with an open manner, with affection and tenderness, the dog will also sense it, and because he knows we are not deceiving him, he is happy to see us. Even animals appreciate frankness in their relations and are hurt by deception.

I believe that in our hearts we have a natural tendency to appreciate straightforwardness and kindness, because every sentient being aspires to happiness and wishes to avoid suffering. What is more, everyone has the right to assure their own happiness and put an end to their suffering. This right belongs to all beings equally. I often express this profound conviction: the meaning, the purpose of human existence is to attain plenitude and happiness. Some may contest this point of view, but I maintain that there are reasons to believe it is correct.

Indeed, although there is absolutely no certainty about what lies ahead, people live with the hope that all will go well for them; they look toward the future with this expectation. The day a person loses hope he risks, if not suicide, at the least falling victim to deep despair and to ruining his life. It is impossible to fulfill our life when we are utterly discouraged. But if we manage to keep our hopes in the future alive, we will be able to overcome all sorts of difficulties and go on living. For all those reasons I think that the goal of our existence is indeed the search for happiness.

I believe that mental happiness is more important and more powerful than physical happiness. What are the causes of mental happiness or suffering? They depend above all on our relations with others. If the people around us regard us favorably, if they are kind to us and let us know their good intentions, our mind will find nourishment and feel very happy. On the other hand, if others treat us with malice or cruelty, we are hurt. Our mind is more at ease in the tenderness and love shown to us by others, and which automatically engender a certain physical ease. The greater our mental happiness, the better our physical well-being. For this reason, I believe that kindness, love, and tenderness are very precious, important attitudes in a person's life.

There are innumerable professions in the sphere of human activity—for example, those dealing with education, law, business, or politics—which may be qualified as beneficial depending upon the attitude or intention displayed in their accomplishment. Whatever path our activity takes, if our intention is that of making ourselves useful to others, there is a good chance our conduct will be useful; whereas activities generally considered to be good, such as the practice of religion, may actually risk causing more harm than good if they are not motivated by the desire to help our fellow beings. Even limited military intervention dictated by an extremely positive and altruistic incentive might prove in the long run to be constructive.

Living as we do, in a modern society, in the midst of great technological development and significant material progress, we risk losing our human values. Because of the mechanization of our lives and the disproportionate consideration, both at work and at home, given to machines (which are, of course, devoid of any human sentiment), human qualities have lost some of their importance. The belief that wealth automatically confers satisfaction and happiness has become very widespread. And yet if we compare the happiness of a person who is relatively impoverished, but lives in a human environment filled with love and kindness, to that of another person who has unlimited wealth but who lives in a difficult environment, surrounded by unfriendly, uncaring people, it becomes obvious that the first person is the happier one.

Whether in terms of character, frame of mind, or lifestyle, it has been shown that children raised in a harmonious, nurturing family environment succeed far better in finding fulfillment than those who grow up in a more difficult, harsher environment where love and affection are lacking.

Our body is not the product of a machine; it functions and develops differently. The material comfort with which we surround ourselves may of course offer the causes and conditions conducive to physical happiness, but as our body is not a machine, all that will not suffice. The factors which contribute to happiness must be cultivated inside us. It is a great error to believe that material conditions alone will suffice for us to be happy; it is from within that we must develop the causes.

This is why I believe that love and affection comprise the fundamental nature, the primordial quality, of human beings. When we show our love, our altruism, we cannot help but feel a certain satisfaction because we are acting in harmony with our own nature. But if we do the opposite, we are going against our basic nature, and this hurts us. Even though our basic nature is good, it remains true that anger, envy, and malice are also aspects of our personality. We can find throughout human history examples of aggression and the desire to do harm expressed in many ways, and this makes some people say that human nature is basically evil and violent—a point of view which is not entirely unjustified. Having said that, if a person were to remain angry twenty-four hours a day he would not live very long, whereas a person whose spirit is constantly filled with love will have a long, happy, and pleasant life. Although greed and malice are part of our spirit, I nevertheless believe the dominant forces within us are love and kindness.

It is important first of all to understand what we mean by love. Love is the desire to see happiness in those who have been deprived of it. We feel compassion toward those who suffer; this is the desire to see them released from their suffering. We habitually feel affection and love for those closest to us and for our friends, but we feel nothing for strangers and even less for those who seek to harm us. This shows that the love for those closest to us is heavily tinged with attachment and desire and that it is partial. Genuine love is not limited to those close to us but extends to all beings, for it is founded on the knowledge that everyone, like us, wishes to find happiness and avoid suffering. Moreover, this extends to all people the right to find happiness and be free of pain. As such, genuine love is impartial and includes everyone without distinction, including our enemies.

As for compassion, we must not confuse it with commiserating pity, for that is tainted with a certain scorn and gives the impression that we consider ourselves superior to those who suffer. True compassion implies the wish to put an end to others' suffering and a sense of responsibility for those who suffer. This sense of responsibility means that we are committed to finding ways to comfort them in their trouble. True love for our neighbor will be translated into courage and strength. As courage grows, fear abates; this is why kindness and brotherly love are a source of inner strength. The more we develop love for others, the more confidence we will have in ourselves; the more courage we have, the more relaxed and serene we will be.

The opposite of love is malice, the root of all faults. On this basis, how can we define an enemy? Generally, we say an enemy is someone who seeks to harm our person or those who are dear to us, or our possessions; someone, therefore, who opposes or threatens the causes of our contentment and our happiness. When an enemy strikes against our belongings, our friends, or our loved ones, he is striking against our most likely sources of happiness. It would be difficult, however, to affirm that our friends and possessions are the true sources of happiness, because in the end the governing factor is inner peace; it is peace of mind that makes us relaxed and happy, and we become unhappy if we lose it.

It is not an external enemy who has the ability to destroy our happiness. In fact, anger, hatred, and malice, if we feel them, are quite apt to destroy our inner peace and in so doing reduce our happiness to nothing. These are our true enemies. Those who know great inner peace remain relaxed and serene even when confronted with the most difficult situations, where everything seems to go against their happiness. But the person whose mind is ravaged by the destructive fires of malice, hatred, and jealousy will know nothing but unhappiness, even under the best circumstances imaginable.

Thus, upon consideration, we find that the true enemy of happiness is to be found within; we cannot designate an actual external enemy. The key to genuine happiness is in our hands. To think about it in this way is to discover the essential values of kindness, brotherly love, and altruism. The more clearly we see the benefits of these values, the more we will seek to reject anything which opposes them; in this way we will be able to bring about inner transformation.

To return to the topic of our discussion, a beneficial act, inspired by altruism, will be a fair and decent act. This brings me to believe that the world's main religions share the goal of reinforcing the fundamental nature of human beings, which is their goodness, and of developing it by various means, according to diverse philosophical views and practices. Thus, at the heart of monotheistic religions such as Christianity, Judaism, or Islam, there is faith in a Creator God. One learns to love God at the same time as one learns to love one's neighbor, but I believe that the main goal common to these spiritual traditions is to learn to love one's neighbor. It is explained that one must love others because God has said to do so; therefore, the more respect one has for God, the more one will listen to his advice, particularly where the necessity for brotherly love is concerned. The essential goal, then, is to encourage people to love each other.

Christianity does not sanction the idea of reincarnation, the concept of successive lifetimes. I have had opportunities to talk about this with a Christian friend, and I told him I saw no incompatibility between the idea of reincarnation and Christian theology. He replied that the problem raised by belief in successive lives was that it would create a certain distance between the believer and God, whereas if one were to accept that God created his or her life, and that this existence is unique, there would be a new element of profound intimacy and greater urgency in one's relationship with God. I can see that his words reflect a certain logic and that his explanation does have substance. In a Christian context, at any rate, this explains the necessity for brotherly love and forgiveness.

Let us now take a look at religions such as Buddhism or Jainism, which do not conceive of a God of creation and consider each individual to be master of his or her destiny: it is up to each person to create the causes of happiness. It is our responsibility, no one else's. If we harm others, we will suffer; if we serve them, we will find happiness. It is in the terms of a law of cause and effect that followers of these traditions explain the necessity of behaving with kindness.

What is the exact relation between ethics and religion? Those who follow a spiritual path consider ethics to be at the base of their quest, which is to avoid hurting others and, on the contrary, treat them with kindness. They explain ethics according to their respective religious beliefs, either, for example, as the will of God, or as the benediction of the Three Jewels (Buddha, his teachings, and the community of practitioners). According to our convictions, we will say that if we follow a particular set of ethics we will go to Heaven or be freed from the cycle of existence.

At the root of all these possible convictions there is, I believe, a universal set of ethics which, in reality, depends upon no particular religion but which can be elaborated and developed within the context of one's chosen tradition. If we adopt this universal morality, upheld by all, if we strengthen and improve it through religious commitment, then our spiritual practice as well as our worldly activities will be in harmony with that set of ethics. Conversely, if we engage in religious practice assiduously but never think of following an ethic of virtuous conduct, nothing good can come of it. It seems essential to me, therefore, that the major religions come to agree upon the importance of a basic set of ethics.

The question arises as to whether such a diversity of spiritual paths is truly necessary if all contain the same essence. Why are there such radically different philosophical and religious views when one unique religion might suffice? I often compare the need for very diverse religions with the variety of food our bodies require. Human beings have different tastes, they appreciate one particular recipe over another, prefer such-and-such a flavor, such-and-such a meal, have a penchant for French, Chinese, or some other cuisine. Everyone prefers to eat according to his or her own personal taste. This is why restaurants generally offer a very wide range of dishes to their patrons; if they were to serve the same dish day after day they would soon go bankrupt!

I believe that the same principle applies where nourishment of the spirit is concerned. To respond to the differing needs of human beings and satisfy their individual dispositions, aspirations, and tendencies, a great variety of philosophies, religions, and spiritual traditions is called for. Given the huge diversity of human needs, it would be extremely difficult for one religion to suffice. The more spiritual paths, the better!

At the same time, it is certain that the different faiths can live in harmony, since the basic, universal morality is an important common ground. It will suffice for the followers of all these different paths to get to know one another better and put what they learn from other religions to good use in order to improve their personal practice. In this way, they will be better able to judge the value of other traditions, and this will in turn lead automatically to greater mutual respect.

When I lived in Tibet, as I did not have any real contact with the representatives of other religions, even though there were Tibetan translations of the Bible, I really believed in my heart of hearts that Buddhism was the best way and I told myself that it would be wonderful if everyone converted to Buddhism. Then, little by little, as I traveled the world, I met representatives of other faiths, people who had a profound experience of their own paths, and who devoted their entire lives either to contemplation or to helping others. The personal contacts and exchanges I had with them led me to recognize the great importance of their religions and to respect them deeply. Of course, Buddhism remains the most precious way to me because it corresponds better to my nature. That does not mean I believe it to be the best religion for everyone. The type of approach that I have just outlined opens the mind and brings great blessings to those who practice it.

Once again, I think it is essential for everyone's happiness that all religions learn to coexist in harmony and mutual respect. When you look at cases as distressing as that of Bosnia where, in the name of religion, human beings are tearing each other apart and causing untold suffering to countless innocent people, you can only feel deep sorrow about such a situation.

In conclusion let us think of a few questions which might spring to mind. For example, say we are sure that the basic nature of sentient beings is good and that developing love for our neighbors will be enough to bring about peace, yet when we look at the history of the world we see nothing but the problems men have created among themselves for thousands of years. How can we believe in the possibility of bringing about universal love? By the same token, can we still hope for harmony and mutual respect between religions when we see that despite common beliefs, they have fought one another throughout history?

My opinion is that it is possible because circumstances have greatly evolved in our modern world. In past times, we could point to the value of altruism and a certain sense of responsibility with regard to others, but we did not necessarily understand the usefulness of such attitudes. Our modern world has developed to such a degree that these two attitudes have now become necessary, if not indispensable. These deep and ancient values have now become crucial. Moreover, because of the rapidity and the importance of exchange and communication between peoples and nations, we are more easily informed of what is going on far from home, and feel therefore closer to those who are far from us physically. This leads to greater solidarity among people. I am convinced that if we try hard enough we can create greater world harmony. That is all I have to say.

Are there limits to compassion? What are the limits of tolerance? What is the difference between acceptance and submission?

I believe I can affirm that compassion knows no limits, as there are no reasons to impose any limits. I imagine that the question is whether we must react and take steps against those who attack us. I think it is possible to react, and at the same time feel compassion toward our aggressors. Steps taken in such a state of mind will be that much more effective. When compassion vanishes and our mind is full of hatred and anger, it founders in confusion. In fact, any measures taken under the influence of such feelings risk going in the wrong direction and will remain ineffective. Hatred must also be distinguished from simple anger; hatred is always reprehensible and never useful, whereas anger may have its usefulness in certain situations. If motivated by compassion, it can enable one to act rapidly; in this case, it becomes constructive.

What, then, is the difference between patience and submission?

True patience means not reacting to the wrongs that are done to us even though we have the means to react, such as when we have the chance to take our revenge and return evil for evil. On the other hand, submission has nothing to do with patience in cases where we are incapable of reacting against the person who is harming us, even though we may be very angry.

Are there women Buddhas?

Of course! Let us take the case of Arya Tara, who was the first woman to attain the spirit of enlightenment, the spontaneous aspiration toward Buddhahood for the good of all beings, and who was a woman. As she entered this spirit of enlightenment, she made this vow: "As there are many who have reached Buddhahood in a masculine form but very few who have done so in a woman's body, and as I have embodied bodhichitta, may I continue along the Way to Enlightenment with a woman's body and become Buddha in a feminine form!" We might conclude that Tara was probably the first feminist in Buddhism!

In the texts of the Vehicles of Perfection (the Paramitayana), and those of the first three classes of the Tantras, it has been said that Buddhahood is generally attained in a masculine form. But according to the fourth class of Tantras, there is no distinction between masculine and feminine; enlightenment may come about just as easily in a woman's body as in a man's.

We all compete with each other, all day long, to get our share of the pie; and yet when we go home in the evening we are supposed to be good and share with our brothers and sisters. How are we to live this contradiction?

Does that mean we encounter no friends during the day? This situation is no doubt very difficult in certain social contexts—when we are obliged to frequent an environment dominated by the spirit of competition. I believe that competition has both positive and negative aspects. For example, we could say that the practice of Buddhism is a sort of constructive competition: our mind is constantly in competition with the negative elements that tend to take over, which it must combat with various antidotes. In the business world and in society at large, there must be room for useful, loyal competition, where intentions are just, where a good example is set. Moreover, we know that a negative form of the competitive spirit is motivated by bad intentions, such as meanness or spite. There also exists a more neutral spirit of competition, particularly in business, in which one endeavors to make profits and earn a living. Everything depends on the mental attitude underlying these activities.

In a society where competition is always present, reactions will vary according to the individual, their nature, and their way of seeing things. If we personally behave in an honest and decent way and are thwarted by others who try to take advantage of our good nature through excessive competititiveness, I believe it is possible to react, without, however, adopting a wrongful attitude; to fail to show a spirit of competition might in such circumstances impede any opportunity for progress.

What is the essential component that parents must include in their children's education?

Whatever the intellectual quality of the education given, for it to be in harmony with fundamental human principles it is vital that it include elements of love and compassion, for nothing guarantees that knowledge alone will be truly useful to human beings. It seems to me that among the major troublemakers society has known there have been many who were well-educated and had great knowledge, but who lacked a moral education, one with an aim to developing compassion, wisdom, and clarity of vision. For this reason it is vital not only to insure children of a high level of knowledge, but also to create a favorable environment for the cultivation of outstanding qualities such as love for others.

How can compassion be taught? Not through words but through acts, by setting an example and acting in such a way that a child will learn by observing his parents; this is why the family environment is so vitally important.

It has been said that laughter is humanity's special gift. In your opinion, do people laugh too much or not enough?

I have been told that certain monkeys have the ability to laugh; I don't know. Whatever the case, it does seem that laughter is indeed particular to human beings. Some people do not smile enough, that is certain! But I do not think one can laugh too much. Who knows? The problem is not so much with those who laugh too much, because they are quite rare, but with those who don't laugh enough, for there are too many of them!

Why is the happiness of some people obtained at the expense of others' happiness?

This stems from a lack of clearsightedness, and holds equally true for those who follow no particular spiritual path. When we seek our own happiness to the detriment of others, at heart we are not truly happy and in the long run we will find ourselves alone, cut off from others.

Our society has reached a high level of scientific and technological knowledge. And yet I still have the impression that our emotions and the stranglehold of violence connected with our greed have not evolved in thousands of years. In your opinion, how could the world resolve this problem without hurting those who are weaker?

In regard to the first part of your question, the problem of violence, I might say that there are a number of factors at play: the two most important being demographic growth, on the one hand; and on the other, the great ease with which weapons can be obtained. To resolve this problem, careful thought must be given to policies of birth control and disarmament. The point is not merely to swamp people's minds with an ever-increasing amount of information, but to make available to everyone on an equal basis the wherewithal to obtain spiritual sustenance, so that they might change their character and improve their behavior toward others. The media, in this case, have a vital role to play; but I do reproach them for focusing too heavily at times on negative events. I think that to give a fairer and more balanced impression of things, the media should give equal emphasis to those events which reflect human qualities and achievements. Otherwise people end up believing that human beings are basically aggressive and bad, and this discourages them.

The second part of the question deals with the violence related to possessiveness. How can this problem be resolved without resorting to destructiveness with regard to those who are weakest? How can wealthy people be encouraged to develop respect for others?

I think all religions encourage the development if not of renunciation, at least of contentment. By showing the benefits of such an attitude they explain how we can be content with little, how we can be content with what we have. I recently visited the monastery of the Grande Chartreuse. It is perhaps rather extreme that these monks live totally cut off from the world, without news from the papers or the radio, yet I was surprised by and filled with admiration for the extraordinary quality of the simplicity of their lives.

How can one learn to be content with few possessions, outside of any religious context? On consideration, are not very rich people slaves to their possessions and their money? Millionaires do not necessarily enjoy a longer life or better health; despite their fortune they are not necessarily any happier than other people. If we remind ourselves of this, we might learn to be satisfied with what we have.

During one of my trips to the United States a very wealthy family invited me to lunch. I observed the opulence and comfort that prevailed in their home and I thought that these people must be completely content. At the end of the meal I went to freshen up in the bathroom. I peeked discreetly into a half-open medicine cabinet: it was full of sleeping tablets and tranquilizers. I concluded that they must not be as happy as they seemed.

Your Holiness, is altruism the opposite of selfishness? Is not a certain measure of selfishness necessary to attain happiness?

To speak of altruism is to explain that we should not be preoccupied with our own welfare. This does not imply that one must become a martyr! What it does mean, simply, is that we should not abandon others and seek solely to find our own happiness, and that we should consider our fellow human beings to be at least as important if not more important than ourselves.

When we are constantly turned toward others in thought as in deed, and try to make them happy, we realize very quickly that our own happiness will follow quite naturally. To cherish others and abandon our own welfare does not mean to suffer. That is why I like to say that if we wish to adopt a selfish attitude, let us at least do it intelligently. I have reasoned it this way: as a rule, we think only of ourselves and forget the rights and aspirations of others, at times to the point of exploiting them for personal gain. In these circumstances, despite our search for happiness we will find nothing but suffering. If, on the other hand, we try to help others by trying to serve them and make them happy, in the end we will gain because we will be happier ourselves. This is what I call intelligent selfishness!

Among the different possible states of mind, some, like desire, are either positive or negative depending on what motivates them. Let us take the case of a very pronounced sense of self: if this is apparent in an attitude of superiority leading to a rejection of and scorn for others, we are dealing with pride, a negative aspect of the mind. But the same notion—this sense of self—may also be expressed by self-confidence, which leads to courage and the assurance of being able, for example, to attain enlightenment for the well-being of all. In this case, it is constructive and positive.

What do you think of passion?

Our commitment and our determination increase when we are passionate. In fact, you can apply this point of view to all emotions, which may, once again, be either negative or positive. Compassion, for example, belongs to the latter category and attachment to the former. Emotions are not in and of themselves positive or negative. If we define passion as an extremely powerful emotion, leading to commitment and to a very intense sense of responsibility, we are in the presence of a truly positive aspect of passion. I once took part in an important meeting of experts where each one spoke at length, analyzing in great detail the realm of his or her specialized knowledge. They were all truly erudite.

When my turn to speak came, I had the impression that there was practically nothing left to say, but all the same I suggested that as a Buddhist psychologist I wanted to emphasize the importance of motivation, of intention—the driving force behind our acts—and of a sense of responsibility. I continued by saying that I feared that with their overly analytical approach, if their house caught on fire, my colleagues would stand there analyzing the situation, wondering how the fire started, where it started, why it was burning in such-and-such a manner, etc. This made everyone laugh!

HUMAN RIGHTS
AND NONVIOLENCE

We speak here of human rights and nonviolence. Personally, I do not view the practice of nonviolence as being merely an act devoid of violence. For me, nonviolence can only be qualified as nonviolent pacifism if it is founded on kindness and altruism. The same applies to human rights.

All human beings have in common the desire to avoid suffering and to know happiness. When our own experience has given us the means to understand that we are not alone in wishing to avoid suffering and live happily, we will be able to develop compassion, the wish to see others free from pain. At the same time, we will be able to experience love, the wish to see all human beings find happiness. These basic concepts should lead us to feel concern about human rights and to take a greater interest in them. I feel, therefore, that respect for human rights and the observance of nonviolence are closely linked to love and compassion.

This quality of altruism is fundamental, in my opinion. It is essential not only for the establishment of good relations among the different world religions, for example, but also to fill our daily lives with serenity and happiness. So I thought I would begin the discussion of these themes by speaking of love.

To get back to our initial topic, whatever our race, education, religion, or standard of living, we are all equal from the day of our birth—we are all human beings and have the same innate desire to avoid suffering and find happiness. Moreover, it is our natural birthright to attain happiness and be free from suffering. But in fact, although all human beings share these desires equally, the nature of society is such that some people enjoy more rights than others, and it is always the poor who are taken advantage of. Whether from a moral or a practical point of view, this is a grave mistake. In fact, the more inequality there is and the more people in need there are in a given society, the greater the social problems that will arise and the more unhealthy that society will be.

To begin with, it is important to understand how much your own happiness is linked to that of others. Human beings are by nature social animals and our happiness depends upon others. If everyone's welfare is assured and a good situation is created overall, the good of the individual will follow as a matter of course. There is no individual happiness totally independent of others. Thus, if we try to assure the well-being of others we will, at the same time, create the conditions for our own well-being.

Human nature is such that the individual is most happy and most relaxed when he or she can share happiness and trust with others. We need the support of our fellows and we like to have friends. When we can laugh with them, we experience a unique pleasure. For myself, I am always happy to meet friends, regardless of whether they are useful to me or not. The fact is that laughter does us a lot of good, quite naturally, and leaves us relaxed. If, however, we turn in upon ourselves and think only of our own person and our own welfare, rejecting, exploiting, and taking advantage of others, our behavior will eventually cut us off from the rest of the world and make us unhappy. So we see that the more we feel concern for others and seek their well-being, the more friends we will have and the more welcome we will feel.

Among our friends there will be some who are attracted by wealth or power, but they are more the friends of our wealth and power than true friends. It is certain that as long as we have wealth and power, such people will hover around us, but the day our situation declines they will vanish like a rainbow, proving their total lack of trustworthiness and loyalty. If we need them and look for them or try to reach them on the phone, for example, well, what a coincidence—these so-called friends are nowhere to be found! If they ever do return our calls, their response is as brief as can be!

To have true friends and be loved by them, we must in turn feel love and sympathy for others. If this is the case, we will automatically have a great number of friends.

If we display an attitude of kindness toward others, and show particular interest in those who are most disadvantaged and those whose rights are not respected, we will establish a basis for our own happiness and truly worthy behavior.

For example, let me speak of my own case, my own experience. I have lost my country and, what is worse, my people have known and still know inconceivable suffering. Tibet itself has been ravaged. I have encountered appalling conditions and had experiences that filled me with deep sorrow. But thanks to my friends and the love which they have shown me I have been able to go on living.

I believe there are several levels of nonviolence. Even with the worst motivation and a mind filled with hypocrisy, falseness, and spite, a person can still speak softly and gently and make friendly gestures, such as giving a gift, for example. This act is nonviolent only in appearance; in reality, it is an act of malevolence. Conversely, we might be motivated by the desire to help someone, to make them aware of their faults, for example, and so we might speak or behave in a somewhat abrupt manner, but at heart the act remains nonviolent.

It is therefore the motivation behind an act that determines whether it is violent or nonviolent. Nonviolent behavior is a physical act or speech motivated by the wish to be useful and helpful. To promote the idea of nonviolence and nonviolent action it is not enough to put an end to violence. We must above all encourage people to foster in themselves an attitude of love and affection for others.

In our era it is necessary to create greater harmony and greater unity among the different world religions. There are already enough factors dividing our society: wealth, politics, etc. Religion is here to help people learn better self-control, to reduce the attachment and antagonism they feel, and to help them find peace. If, however, religion becomes a pretext for even more attachment, hatred, or sectarianism, this is a lamentable state of affairs.

Of course, each religion has its own characteristics. On a metaphysical level there are even great differences between religions. Two major groups can be distinguished: religions which adhere to a belief in the concept of a Creator, and those which do not. Regarding philosophical views, this is an enormous difference. However, all major religions agree on the importance of love, patience, and tolerance. Although each may present the exact nature of that love in a somewhat different fashion, all do insist on the necessity of love and kindness, and all counsel their followers in various ways to nurture these feelings. Thus there is already significant common ground among the religions of the world.

Given the fact that one of the principal sources of harmony among religions is the universality of precepts about love, the sooner we recognize the purpose of this love and its precious nature, the greater the respect we will feel for religions other than our own.

Everyday happiness depends greatly on our state of mind. Days when we feel calm will be happy days. But on days where our serenity is absent, we will be unhappy. This is clear.

Now, what is the purpose of life? I generally say that it is happiness. Why? Because even those who follow a spiritual path do so only in order to find happiness. They see religion as the best method for attaining happiness, and that is why they follow a spiritual path. In the same way, a person who works in the area of the economy (or in any other field, for that matter) does so in principle because he or she feels that it is the best, most useful thing for a life of fulfillment.

Although we know nothing for certain about the future, nearly everyone thinks that things will get better. Despite the various problems we encounter in a lifetime, we continue to hope that everything will go well in the future. The day we cease to hope we are in danger of becoming depressed or even of committing suicide. That is why I think that the search for happiness is what gives meaning to our lives.

There are people who define happiness in terms of material or external circumstances; wealth or great power signifies happiness. It is true that having a certain material comfort, having friends and family close by, enjoying a good reputation and good conversations, are a number of factors that contribute to our happiness. But if these were the main causes of happiness, it would necessarily follow that all those who enjoy wealth, renown, and agreeable surroundings would be happy. But this is hardly the case! This goes to show that although such favorable conditions may contribute to our happiness, they are not its fundamental cause, nor are they indispensable to it.

Regardless of whether people enjoy good material circumstances, if they have peace of mind, are relaxed and at ease in themselves, it can be said of them that they are happy. The reverse holds equally true. Thus, it is clear that inner peace is the principle cause of happiness. We can observe this in our daily lives. On days when we are calm and happy, even if difficulties arise or we fall victim to a mishap, we take it well, it doesn't bother us unduly. But on days when we feel sad or have lost our usual calmness, the least little annoyance will take on enormous proportions and be deeply upsetting to us.

In general it would appear at first glance that the developed countries of the West have all the conditions offered by modern life and that as a result they are wonderful in every respect. But if you take the time for a quiet discussion with the inhabitants of these countries, you find that they are plagued by doubt, misconceptions, anxiety, jealousy, and competitiveness.

So how can one recover contentment of the mind? By taking drugs or drinking? Certainly not! By complaining to a doctor, as we would for a physical illness: "Doctor, I'm suffering morally, find me a cure!" The doctor will surely reply by shaking his head that there is nothing he can do for us, and will send us elsewhere. In short, happiness is something we must create from within. The question that arises is: how do we do this? What is the best way to find this happiness?

To give an answer based on my own experience, a number of my friends and I have reached the same conclusion: the more we develop love and affection for others, and the desire to serve them, the more our own state of mind will find serenity. When we wish to help others, our attitude toward them is more positive. We are not jealous of them and we feel less need to hide things from them. We feel we can allow ourselves to be less reserved, more open, in their presence. Conversely, if deep within we nurture harmful thoughts of jealousy and malevolence in our relations with others, we will remain at a distance and be isolated; naturally, we will always be on the periphery of things.

When we seek to help others, our relations with them become easier. Otherwise we remain shy and hesitant, and feel the need to take a thousand precautions before we approach them. In wanting to help others we will be less afraid and have less anxiety. When our intentions are good, we have greater self-confidence and are stronger. In this way, we learn to understand how precious kindness is, how valuable it is to us. Now, how can we engender kindness?

Everyone, whatever their situation, has a natural ability to produce compassion from within. From the very day of our birth when we drink our mother's milk, this compassion arises within us. This act is a symbol of love and affection. If the child did not feel close to his mother he would not feed; and if the mother did not feel such great love for her child, did not cherish it, she would surely have no milk to give him. I think this act from the very first day of life establishes the basis of our entire life.

Everyone agrees that a child who grows up in a family environment full of love and affection has a greater chance to feel content within himself, to study well and have a happy life; while a child who has lacked affection throughout his childhood is distracted in his studies. Because of this lack of emotional support during his growing years he will have a tendency to have problems all his life.

At the end of life, at the moment of death, the dying man must leave his loved ones. Although he knows it serves no purpose, he is nevertheless happy to have a close friend near him. For this reason I think that from our birth to our last day, throughout our life, the need to give and experience love and affection is fundamental.

Our state of mind can even influence our physical state and the functioning of the cells which make up our body. When our mind is relaxed and at ease, our circulation, for example, is normal; our physical organism works well and ages less quickly. If we are anxious or angry, on the other hand, this psychological tension will upset the equilibrium of the various elements in our body and may even lead to high blood pressure. The body of an unhappy person ages more quickly. A troubled mind does nothing for one's physical well-being, whereas a relaxed state of mind suits the body perfectly.

Once we have observed all the advantages of kindness, we should seek to cultivate it. At the same time, if we look at the harm caused by the emotions opposite to kindness, such as anger, spite, or especially hatred, we should seek to refute them and prevent them from ever becoming part of us.

Everyone likes their friends and dislikes their enemies. But what is an enemy? An enemy is someone who tries to hurt us, our body, our belongings, our family, and our friends—in short, anything which brings us happiness. We might consider our belongings, our reputation, our friends, our family, and so forth, to be the ordinary sources of happiness, and whoever wrongs those sources is an ordinary enemy.

The principal source of happiness is inner peace. Someone who has already had practice in developing this peace, who already has a certain experience of it, will not be easily troubled by ordinary enemies. However, hatred, malice, and spite will immediately destroy this mental calmness. The true enemy, therefore, is malice. External enemies may be real enemies for a certain time, but it is quite conceivable that one day instead of harming us they may turn into friends. But the inner enemy will always be our enemy—in the beginning, midway through, and at the end; it is impossible that it will ever become useful to us. Consequently, it is totally illogical and contradictory to seek happiness on the one hand, yet leave room on the other for spite and malice to remain within us, for these are the primary agents seeking to destroy our happiness.

How can we annihilate this enemy we call hatred? The direct remedy for aversion is patience, the practice of patience. It is primarily when we feel uneasy, prey to some moral suffering, that we have a reaction of aversion. Thus, to avoid feeling aversion we must behave in such a way that we feel no moral pain. We must do everything possible to avoid suffering; suffering must be prevented. It is therefore very important to transform any situation, be it good or bad, into an opportunity to improve. When something bad happens to us and we were not expecting it, an illness for example, if we think only of ourselves, the difficulty will take on enormous proportions and the event will seem totally unfair. But if we think of others, of their problems, even for a moment, we will see that our situation is in no way exceptional.

The notion of what constitutes a problem is completely relative. It is possible to see a positive aspect of any difficulty. A given situation may be viewed at the same time either as unbearable or as beneficial. It all depends on how we look at it. In any case, we must make certain that things do not begin to seem unbearable to us. When we have problems, if we look at them too closely we will see nothing else and they will begin to appear all out of proportion with reality; this is when they become intolerable. But if we can stand back from them, we will be better able to judge them and they will seem less serious.

To better understand the damaging effects of rejecting other people and the benefits of caring for them, it is a good idea to stop and reflect from time to time in the following manner. Let us step back from ourselves, become an outside observer or third party to, in one example, a group of people in need; and in another example, our usual, ordinary selves—that is, someone who is completely self-centered, who does not care about other people. As we observe ourselves in this manner we will gradually come to see more clearly the fault of selfishness and, without realizing it, our inner gaze will turn automatically to the group of people in need.

If we practice thinking in this way, we will automatically begin to better understand the negative effects of caring only for ourselves and the benefits of caring for others. Subsequently, this will allow us to reduce the strength of our attachment and aversion and to develop love and consideration for others. Thanks to this practice, a gradual transformation will take place within us. But we must be careful— we must not think that the change will be instantaneous, like switching on a light! Bearing this in mind, it is important to give ourselves time, to practice slowly and progressively.

I think that attempting in this way to develop more love and compassion in ourselves and to reduce anger and spite is a universal spiritual activity which requires no faith in any religion whatsoever. In fact, it seems wrong to me to believe that kindness is exclusively the business of religion and that it must be neglected if one is not interested in spirituality. Everyone has the right to practice or not practice religion, but as long as we seek happiness and continue to live in a society, love and affection are indispensable.

In conclusion, I would like to say that the very root of respect for human rights and nonviolence is love and kindness to others.

Is violence solely a human matter? Is it instinctive, is it in human nature? When does a human being have a right to be violent—in what case is it a strength?

Of course violence is part of human nature, but that nature has many sides and I do not think violence is one of the more important aspects. At our birth we are naturally ignorant of everything, but over the years as we study our ignorance decreases. So we change the initial situation. In the same way, we are born with aversion and aggressiveness, but with practice we can and must also change this.

You asked if on occasion aggression could be justified. I think first of all that we must make a distinction between anger and hatred. Anger may at times have a positive side, a usefulness in cases where it brings about a quick response. But in general I think that anger is a sign of weakness and tolerance a sign of strength.

What is forgiveness?

Forgiveness? It is very precious, very important! But it does not mean simply closing your eyes and forgetting the wrong that has been done to you; you must remember it. But love and respect for others, among other reasons, must keep you from returning the wrong done to you. This is very important.

Do Tibetan children still manage to follow Buddhist teachings?

There are those who manage and others who do not. It all depends to a great extent on their family environment.

To what degree do you think being Christian is compatible with being Buddhist?

I think it is quite possible. There are also things Buddhists can learn from the experience of our Christian brothers and sisters. Recently, during a visit to a Catholic monastery, I found that the monks I met there had many things in common with Tibetan Buddhists. With some aspects, such as poverty and contentment, I find the ways of the Christian monks to be better than those of our own monks. I think some Tibetan monks have perhaps a bit too much comfort. Just as Tibetan monks could learn a few things in this respect from Christian monks, Christian followers could in turn learn certain techniques for developing love, compassion, one-pointed concentration, and for improving altruism, from their Tibetan counterparts. I think with these topics it is possible to borrow those techniques specific to Buddhism, and I have Christian friends who do this. When different religions come together, there is a great deal they can learn from each other.

Don't you think that nonviolence could lead to the extermination of your people?

Nonviolence is the best method in the long run, the most profound. For example, thanks to the nonviolent path Tibet has chosen there are now more and more Chinese who support the Tibetan cause.

Your Holiness, what advice would you give to lay followers so that they might progress toward kindness and compassion?

First of all, we must recognize the great capacity we all have within. In Buddhism we speak of the Buddhanature present in each individual. But without going into that, as human beings we have certain emotions, such as determination or intelligence; the combination of these two offers many possibilities. It is important to ally our intelligence with good intention. Without intelligence we cannot accomplish very much. Without good intentions, we will not know whether the exercise of our intelligence is constructive or destructive. That is why it is important to have a good heart. Let us not forget that all these qualities are part of our basic nature.

A RELIGIOUS DUTY

Do you believe that the separation of church and state is a good thing? Do you think that more encouragement should be given for the possibility that churches should call on the state and intervene actively in areas which concern society as a whole, such as the environment?

As far as the institutions are concerned I think it is desirable for state and church to operate separately. That does not mean, however, that the church should not give its opinion from a spiritual point of view or become actively involved where the environment is concerned, for this is an issue concerning the welfare of the entire population.

After all, the very purpose of religion and its practice is to serve humanity. It is therefore the duty of religious people to step in and try to solve certain social problems. It is truly very useful for a person to temper his or her politics with a spiritual approach. I once took part in a conference with politicians in India. They admitted quite humbly that as politicians they were very ignorant about religion. I replied that politicians should be even more religious, given the repercussions of their acts upon society. In fact, the thoughts of a hermit who devotes himself entirely to contemplation do not have a large-scale effect on the population. But the corruption deriving from the disturbed mind of a politician and the ensuing scandal will harm a considerable number of people.

Is it difficult for you, spending as much time as you do in meditation, to be living presently in the midst of such media madness?

As long as these encounters take place in an atmosphere of warm human feelings, they do not bother me in the least—on the contrary, I enjoy them a great deal! Any exchange between human beings devoid of human warmth or human feeling is like a conversation between machines, and I'm not interested. Of course, I begin my day very early, before dawn, at four in the morning. That is why I am often tired and sleepy during the evening.

PART III

NONVIOLENCE: AN EXAMPLE TO FOLLOW

I AM ONLY A SIMPLE BUDDHIST MONK and, if I could follow my inclinations, I would seek refuge in the solitude of the mountains like
a wounded deer. But, as it happens, I was given the name of Dalai
Lama as well as the job that goes with it, and the Tibetan people have
placed great hope in me. Is this due to my karma or to prayers I have
made in the past?

Whatever the case may be, as a Tibetan I naturally feel concerned
by anything having to do with my country, which is at present going
through one of the most difficult periods of its history. For over forty
years Tibet has known a time of great suffering. You have the good
fortune of being able to express an interest in your own history and
culture and of being able to enjoy them in total liberty. That is not
the case in Tibet. I am therefore at present invested with an immense
moral responsibility, and not only toward the people of Tibet. I also
have the duty, whenever I encounter someone who is interested in
Tibet, to explain the situation clearly and give an indication of what
we are doing to resolve the problem.

The old Tibetan society was not perfect. It was a society of farming and herding which relied primarily on serf labor. Still, if we compare it to those societies prevalent at the same time in India and China,
ours was not as harsh and showed greater compassion. I think a number of ancient civilizations, the Indians of the Americas for example,
showed this same great respect for the earth, nature, trees. In Tibetan
culture the relation to nature, including animals, was extremely peaceful; we lived in harmony with nature. When Buddhism came to Tibet,
the society was in general permeated with more compassion and openness. It was a society in which people felt at ease and which to this

day harbors a great wealth of traditions capable of comforting the majority of those who suffer from deep inner afflictions. Moreover, this society certainly has a great deal to say about current problems, such as the environment or violence. As a result, the preservation of Tibetan culture and traditions is not the responsibility of a few thousand Tibetans alone, but concerns the entire world.

TIBET

BETWEEN RESISTANCE AND NONVIOLENCE

Your Holiness, what Westerners most often know about Buddhism is the principle of reincarnation, but we do not always manage to understand it. Would it be possible for you to explain to us what reincarnation consists of?

There exist, of course, many religions and spiritual traditions in our world and they can be roughly divided into two categories: those which believe in reincarnation, that is, a succession of lives; and those which do not. For the first category, it is certain that the aggregate of form—the gross human body—is limited to one life and is the owner of that life. The individual, the self or the flow of consciousness, is perpetuated from existence to existence.

When we speak of the flow of consciousness, what do we mean by consciousness? Consciousness is not a simple, unique entity. There are different levels of consciousness: gross, subtle, and extremely subtle. Gross consciousness is that which is associated with our body, with the physical aggregate, during our life; it is most certainly that which can be identified as localized, for example, in the brain, assuring the functioning of different corporal activities. It is the most obvious and the easiest to grasp; it is also that which disappears along with our body when we die.

But there is also a more subtle consciousness which has no material support or material connection to the gross body. It is this, we believe, that will continue after the body has ceased to exist, after death. If we try to understand the origins of this subtle consciousness, it seems that it cannot appear out of nowhere, and that it requires a cause that is of the same nature as itself—that is, an instant of preceding consciousness. If we wish to return to the original instant of this consciousness, we will not be able to do so because that would presuppose that such a consciousness is born at a given moment, or is produced by something inanimate. That is why when speaking of consciousness we say that it has no inception. An instant of consciousness can be born of no other cause than one which resembles it: another instant of consciousness, not something inanimate. This is how we understand reincarnation in Buddhism.

The Dalai Lama is traditionally considered to be the reincarnation of his predecessor. If we follow this principle, is it possible that one day the Dalai Lama will be a woman rather than a man, or a non-Tibetan rather than a Tibetan?

It is conceivable; both are possible. The fourth Dalai Lama, Yonten Gyatso, was a Mongol. The first time in the history of Tibet where there was formal, we might say official, recognition of the incarnation of a deceased lama was with the First Karmapa Rinpoche, a great Tibetan lama. Around the same time, a lineage of reincarnations of a great sage began, a woman called Samding Dorje Pamo, who continued to be reborn all through the history of Tibet. This woman was recognized for her high degree of spiritual realization, and she also occupied an important position in the Tibetan spiritual hierarchy.

So if the feminist movement continues to develop, there may some day be a woman Dalai Lama! There are no theoretical obstacles.

You have stated publicly that you envision giving up this method of designating your successor. Why is this, and what would you replace it with?

From the beginning of our struggle to liberate our country, certain sources have been trying to distort our ideas. These sources have tried to propagate the belief that our struggle seeks only to restore the old system to power. In reality this is not at all the case. We have only been refugees since 1959, and in 1962 we had already begun the process of democratizing Tibetan society. I put together a small committee whose task was to draw up a constitution for the future Tibet. I had a clause added to the constitution according to which a two-thirds majority of the assembly could do away with the office of the Dalai Lama. In 1969 I made an official declaration according to which the office of the Dalai Lama and its survival would depend entirely upon the will of the Tibetan people. In one of the propositions I made concerning the future of Tibet, I made it very clear that in a future Tibet I will not hold political office and that the government will be democratically elected by the people. If the institution of the Dalai Lama is no longer appropriate in the future, it will cease to exist.

You have often stated that Buddhism, like Christianity, Judaism, or Islam, is one of the world's great religions. But at other times you have also stated that Buddhism is not really a religion. Would you clarify this contradiction for us?

First of all, if we adhere to the definitions given by certain dictionaries, which state that religion necessarily implies belief in a Creator God, then, indeed, we may say that Buddhism is not a religion. This is why certain scholars and scientists also consider Buddhism to be more a science of the mind.

But if we define a religion, in this case Buddhism, as a spiritual practice of prayer and meditation seeking a result in the afterlife, what we call nirvana, for example, then in that case we can say that Buddhism is indeed a religion. It is a religion, a philosophy, and a science at the same time.

I would like to add that the relationship between those religions based almost exclusively upon faith, where there is little room for reason, and the most down-to-earth materialism is very difficult. Buddhism, I believe, is situated somewhere between these two extremes. From the point of view of the radical materialists, Buddhism is considered a religion and as such has no place in their system of thought. From the point of view of religions based primarily on faith and belief, Buddhism is not considered a religion but rather a type of atheism, or science of the mind. For those reasons it is also set aside. Buddhism is therefore somewhere in between, which may allow it to be a bridge between the two extremes.

Despite the extreme cultural differences, more and more Westerners in search of spirituality are turning to Buddhism rather than Christianity. How do you explain this?

I do not think we should generalize too quickly, because Western countries are predominantly Christian countries and likely to remain so. Tibet, for example, is an essentially Buddhist country, but for centuries there have also been non-Buddhists there, Muslims, among others, and since the early part of this century there have also been some Christians. So in the same way I think that among the millions of Westerners it is normal to find a few attracted to the ideas of Buddhism.

Conversely, can Tibetans benefit from Christianity?

Of course! From what I know of Christianity, there is an abundance of excellent traditions, and I have met Christian monks and nuns who impressed me deeply by the way in which they have taken on great responsibilities in the realms of education and health care — they really do serve humanity, all over the world. Another very positive aspect of the Christian tradition is, I believe, the fact that the novitiate is so long and rigorous, and that the monks are given time to consider carefully before they choose to become fully ordained. Where Buddhists are concerned, I think there are sometimes too many monks who become fully ordained before they have really thought about it.

The Catholic Church, through the Pope, has spoken out quite radically on certain social issues, in particular sexuality. For example, the Church condemns abortion or the use of condoms in the fight against AIDS. Do you have a position on these issues?

As far as the question on abortion is concerned, Buddhism holds each human life to be infinitely precious. From this point of view it is advised to avoid birth control. Given demographic expansion and the limited quality of resources, the question now arises: can five billion human beings be happy? The widening gap between the standards of living of the countries of the North and the South is not only unjust on a moral level but also on a practical level. It is a source of problems and suffering and requires serious thought. According to experts, if the standard of living of the countries of the South were brought up to that of the North, the world's resources would no longer suffice. This analysis is based on scientific data. The only conclusion is that new births must be limited.

To return to abortion: in general, abortion means killing and is therefore a negative act. But there can be exceptional cases, such as, for example, when the fetus is deformed or the life of the mother is in danger—but these are exceptions. That is the Buddhist position and that is why I personally advocate nonviolent methods of contraception. I am also fond of pointing out that the best means of nonviolent contraception would be to have more monks and nuns!

One of the major debates dividing the Catholic Church concerns the celibacy of priests, but this practice also exists in Tibetan Buddhism. Is monastic celibacy essential, in your opinion?

In very many religions and spiritual traditions celibacy is considered to be a very important factor. It is a purely personal choice, of course, and one is free to make it or not.

Buddhism realizes that the major causes of suffering are passions, mental factors which disturb and confuse our mind. Among these negative mental factors, the most active and the most harmful are aversion and attachment. The harmful effects of aversion and hatred are obvious to everyone. But attachment and desire often develop along with a reaction of aversion. One of the main goals of spiritual practice is to find remedies for the factors that disturb the mind— aversion and attachment. There are various types of attachment, and those linked to the experiences of the five senses cause great suffering to human beings. One of the most obvious is attachment to sexual pleasure. So this is why Buddhism praises the virtues of chastity and abstinence, and discourages any form of sexual misconduct.

BEING AND REMAINING TIBETAN

Your Holiness, you have accused the Chinese of seeking to destroy Tibetan culture. How are they going about it, and in your opinion will they be able to attain their goal?

From the time of the occupation, forty years ago, the Chinese have used diverse methods at different times. Since the mid-Fifties they have destroyed countless monasteries and temples; they have eliminated educated people, lay followers as well as monks, by imprisoning them, sending them to labor camps, or even executing them in public. Then there was the Cultural Revolution; I think everyone has heard of that. Finally, there was propaganda claiming that Tibetan culture is completely backward and obscure; it was said to be cruel and worthless, and that everything Tibetan was completely useless and uninteresting. I think they no longer use these methods.

In the methods used now, since the mid-Eighties, the official position is that Tibetan culture is an ancient culture, worthy of interest, which must be preserved. The Chinese have put some signs in Tibetan up in the streets and they have even ordered Chinese people living in Tibet to learn Tibetan. But underneath all of this the emphasis remains on Chinese studies, and in school examinations, for example, it is one's knowledge of China that matters. The traditional Tibetan degree course is very serious and very long, requiring twenty or thirty years of study to complete. Now there is almost no place in Tibet where these studies may be taken from beginning to end. There may still be some very tiny remote regions where it can be done without the Chinese authorities knowing about it. As a result, the level of our traditional instruction in Tibet has dropped very low. For this very reason thousands of young people have no other choice than to come to India to study at the monastic institutions set up in exile.

So, despite all the propaganda one hears, the reality is that there has been a deliberate effort to eliminate our culture. And it is primarily due to the invasion of Chinese colonists that cultural genocide is now occuring in Tibet, whether it is deliberate or not.

I can give you an example. Quite recently a Tibetan who lives in India went to see his parents in Tibet. As he was walking in the old quarter of Lhasa where the Tibetans live, around the central temple, he was surprised to see that everyone was dressed like the Chinese, speaking Chinese. At one point he deliberately shouted out in Tibetan. When he saw several people react to his cry, he went up to them and asked them why they were speaking Chinese. They answered that if they did not speak Chinese, the Chinese would scorn them, whereas when they spoke Chinese they felt they were more on an equal footing with them.

Your Holiness, how do you feel about those who are the cause of your people's suffering?

I sometimes feel rather irritated, but as a practicing Buddhist, upon reflection, there are more reasons to feel concern for the one who creates the problem, who causes others to suffer. There is more reason for concern for the aggressor than for the victim. Why is this? Because the one who causes problems sets in motion an entire karmic process which will bring him negative consequences in the future, even if it is a very distant future; whereas the victim is already suffering the consequence of a negative action in the past. For the victim, the result ends there. If I think in this manner I am able to develop true compassion for those people.

Is there a danger that the different lifestyles of Tibetans in exile and those who have remained in Tibet may create a cultural rift between these two groups?

No, I do not think there will be a problem. Obviously, those who live in India do have a somewhat different life, different knowledge as well, because they have access to information about the outside world. So there are obvious differences. Despite our status as refugees we enjoy total liberty. But there are only 130,000 of us, whereas there are 6 million in Tibet. That is why I always say that they are the leaders, they are my boss. They are many, we are only a small element of the equation. I do not think there will be any problem in the future. Obviously it is possible that at the time of returning to Tibet some will find it hard to live there and may prefer to remain outside, but that will not be a problem.

What have your ties with the Western world brought you, personally?

Since childhood I have always been fascinated by material progress and Western technology. What always strikes me with Western people is their fervent desire to learn. Every time I give a talk about Buddhism, for example, you all get out your pencils and paper to take notes, or turn on tape recorders. Tibetans, Chinese, and Indians, I have noticed, may listen to me with great devotion, but no one gets out a pen. They sit there calmly, as if they already knew everything!

I have always admired a genuine scientific attitude in research, where impartiality, open-mindedness, and even skepticism play an important part. There is a similar approach in Buddhism, generally speaking, more particularly in the Great Vehicle, the Mahayana, where it is said to accept nothing blindly. Everything must be experienced and verified. Only when things become clear and convincing should one accept them. This is what I find positive in the West.

But if you were to ask me what the negative things are . . . I cannot say that this is true for all Westerners, but I sometimes find that my friends lack patience. I wonder if that is not due to the fact that you are all used to automatic machines and that you can do everything very easily. So you are spoiled. That does not stop patience from being something very useful in human life. In the West, when it comes time to judge the quality of something, there is perhaps a tendency to forget that everything is relative. You cannot say of a thing that it is 100 percent black or 100 percent white, 100 percent good or 100 percent bad. Things are not so clear-cut: everything has a positive and negative side. All we can do to be practical and realistic is to consider things which are mostly positive as good, and those which are mostly negative as bad.

With the hindsight of experience, how do you see, today, the Tibet of before 1950?

I think there were certainly drawbacks and a certain backwardness, but there were also positive aspects. Some people used to describe the old Tibet as a kind of Shangri-la, a paradise, which is obviously an exaggeration. Others would describe it as hell on earth, which is also an exaggeration.

The more I encounter the diverse people and cultures of our world, the more I realize just how much Tibetan civilization is an ancient one, rich and refined, and how much it contributes to the preservation of inner peace, which is very positive. This is probably because Tibetan culture, founded on the teachings of Buddha, fostered a harmonious and peaceful relationship with the environment. Although Tibetans are not vegetarians, they protect wild animals, fish, and birds. In the old days there were even government decrees which forbade hunting, fishing, and the killing of birds. I believe that only a few Gurkhas, who were Nepalese, were exempt from this; as they did not come under Tibetan jurisdiction, they could fish and hunt. Tibetans did not, at least in central Tibet, and I think that was very good. At the time we did not know what "environment" and "ecology" meant, but we put these measures into practice spontaneously.

Even where the social system was concerned, outmoded and feudal as it was, compared to what was in India and China at the time it was much less harsh, much kinder. For example, at that time in China it was common practice to bind women's feet and to make some people into eunuchs. These practices did not exist in Tibet.

THE FUTURE OF A FREE TIBET

Your Holiness, in a 1988 speech you relinquished the demand for Tibetan independence in order to facilitate the opening of negotiations with the Chinese. Was this, to your way of thinking, a definitive renunciation?

As I said earlier, Tibet is threatened with extinction. We must therefore do everything possible to save this country with its unique cultural heritage. The political reality is that no one will come to chase the Chinese out. The only realistic attitude is to deal directly with the Chinese government. Our strength is justice and truth. We have no reason to hide; we have every right, and the necessary fortitude, to go to our Chinese brothers and sisters and confront them.

At the end of 1978 the Chinese government made it known that it wanted to establish contact with me. I immediately responded and sent a special personal envoy, one of my brothers who speaks Chinese well. He met with Deng Xiaoping. They conferred for an hour and Deng Xiaoping told him that could talk about everything except total independence, but that was a considerable condition.

Since then, in the fourteen years which have followed, my entire approach has been based on that condition. That is why I do not ask for complete independence. That does not mean that we do not have the right to demand independence. Everyone now knows that Tibet is an occupied country. I generally refer to my way of proceeding as the Middle Way. I stated very clearly in my proposition at Strasbourg that the final decision belongs to the Tibetan people themselves. Some Tibetans were very critical of this proposition, some going so far as to say to me, "You, the Fourteenth Dalai Lama, have sold the birthright of the Tibetan people!" But I think we must face the situation squarely:

Tibet is a landlocked country; to gain access to the sea we are obliged to rely on a neighboring country. In the present context, it seems fairer and more realistic to try and come up with an arrangement or a solution with the Chinese.

A considerable portion of Tibetan territory has been redistributed to neighboring Chinese provinces. What do you think the borders of the future autonomous Tibet should be?

In the seventh century, the border between Tibet and China was drawn up very clearly. The Chinese government has tried to use all sorts of historical arguments with references to the thirteenth century and the seventh century. . . . Given the fact that I accepted the first condition set down by Mr. Deng Xiaoping, I feel I have every right to discuss the rest of the issue. So I told them that since the Chinese government itself recognizes the existence of all sorts of regions, districts, zones, and even counties which the government itself calls ethnic Tibetan zones, counties, and districts, why not regroup them all together as one single entity? This would make it much simpler and much easier to preserve and protect Tibetan culture and identity. Already in the eighth century, during the reign of King Trisong Detsen and King Tri Ralpachen, the border between China and Tibet had been clearly demarcated from the Chinese province of Yunnan to the Tibetan province of Amdo, in the north. There are inscriptions, some of them on pillars, others on rocks. In Yunnan province, for example, there are rock carvings. These ancient inscriptions indicate the true border between China and Tibet, and this is not something we have made up, but historical reality.

All authoritarian regimes in general, and Communist regimes in particular, have an unfortunate tendency to distort history by rewriting it. I saw this very clearly when I went to China in 1954 and 1955. I spent roughly six months in China proper, then I visited Manchuria, which the Chinese call Tumbe, and also the regions of Hreang and Heilongjang. There I saw a museum of Japanese atrocities, where it was explained that the Japanese only surrendered once the Soviet army had destroyed the Japanese army division in Manchuria, the Quang-tuong army. I was in Lhasa at that time, and there we learned what had really happened—in fact, the Japanese surrendered only after the atomic bombing of Hiroshima and Nagasaki, and Russia declared war on Japan after the bombs were dropped. The Chinese version claims that the Japanese surrendered only after the Russians had anni-hilated the most powerful Japanese army in Manchuria. This is an example of the distortion of history.

You have often stated that you would like to achieve a synthesis between Buddhism and Marxism. What is the appeal of Marxism for you?

Of all the modern economic theories, the economic system of Marx-ism is founded on moral principles, while capitalism is concerned only with gain and profitability. Marxism is concerned with the dis-tribution of wealth on an equal basis and the equitable utilization of the means of production. It is also concerned with the fate of the working classes—that is, the majority—as well as with the fate of those who are underprivileged and in need, and Marxism cares about the victims of minority-imposed exploitation. For those reasons the system appeals to me, and it seems fair. I just recently read an article in a paper where His Holiness the Pope also pointed out some posi-tive aspects of Marxism.

As for the failure of the Marxist regimes, first of all I do not con-sider the former USSR, or China, or even Vietnam, to have been true Marxist regimes, for they were far more concerned with their narrow national interests than with the Workers' International; this is why there were conflicts, for example, between China and the USSR, or between China and Vietnam. If those three regimes had truly been based upon Marxist principles, those conflicts would never have occurred.

I think the major flaw of the Marxist regimes is that they have placed too much emphasis on the need to destroy the ruling class, on class struggle, and this causes them to encourage hatred and to neglect compassion. Although their initial aim might have been to serve the cause of the majority, when they try to implement it all their energy is deflected into destructive activities. Once the revolution is over and the ruling class is destroyed, there is not much left to offer the people; at this point the entire country is impoverished and unfortunately it is almost as if the initial aim were to become poor. I think that this is due to the lack of human solidarity and compassion. The principal disadvantage of such a regime is the insistence placed on hatred to the detriment of compassion.

The failure of the regime in the former Soviet Union was, for me, not the failure of Marxism but the failure of totalitarianism. For this reason I still think of myself as half-Marxist, half-Buddhist.

You have called for the repatriation of the Chinese who now live in Tibet. Might there be a place for a Chinese population in a democratic, open Tibet?

I think we should differentiate the various groups of Chinese living in Tibet. There are, on the one hand, those who were already there in 1949; then all those who went there or were sent in compliance with official plans; and, finally, those who have been coming since the so-called "liberal economic policy," and who come on their own initiative, as individuals. We should also distinguish the Chinese who speak Tibetan and respect Tibetan culture—for, after all, Buddhist culture is not so foreign to them—from all those who come to Tibet merely in search of material wealth and not spiritual wealth. Those who respect Tibetan spirituality could prove themselves to be very beneficial if they stay. If there are not too many of them I see no reason why we could not work it out so that they can remain in Tibet. But as for all those who think that Tibetans are backward and barbarian, that they are dirty and smell bad (we think in turn that the Chinese smell bad, that they eat too much garlic), it would be better if they went home. Why should they stay in a place if they think it is dirty?

THE STRUGGLE FOR FREEDOM

Your Holiness, in your struggle to liberate Tibet, do you absolutely refuse the use of violence, or is nonviolence for you simply the best way to attain your goal?

Yes, I absolutely refuse the use of violence. For several years now I have been asked on several occasions what I would do if the despair of certain Tibetans drove them to violence, and I have always replied that if that were to happen I would give up and step back. I have reasons for thinking in this way; it is not merely a blind belief. First of all, I believe that the basic nature of human beings is gentle and compassionate. It is therefore in our own interest to encourage that nature, to make it live within us, to leave room for it to develop. If on the contrary we use violence, it is as if we voluntarily obstruct the positive side of human nature and prevent its evolution.

The First World War ended with the defeat of Germany, and this defeat left a deep trauma in the German people. That is how the seeds of the Second World War were sown. Once violence gains the upper hand in a situation, emotions can no longer be controlled. This is dangerous and leads to tragedy. This is exactly what is happening in Bosnia at the moment. Violent methods merely create new problems.

In our case, what is most important is the fact that we Tibetans and our Chinese brothers and sisters have always been neighbors and must remain so. The only alternative for the future is to learn to get along and live in harmony with our neighbors. We must seek a solution between the Chinese and the Tibetans that will offer mutual benefits. Because of our nonviolent attitude, Chinese people both within China and abroad have already expressed sympathy and concern for our cause; some have even said they greatly appreciate our nonviolent attitude.

Would you have also refused to take up arms against Hitler?

I don't know. We have to go into a bit of detail. At the time Nazism was taking root and beginning to gain strength and importance, I would personally have made every effort to stop it, if I could have at the time.

Not long ago, when I was in Poland, I visited the camp at Auschwitz where thousands of innocent people were exterminated. I stayed for a moment in the gas chamber and when I saw the crematorium I was filled with profound sadness. The worst was when I came upon the piles of shoes and human hair. In the middle of all those shoes were little children's shoes; they had been patched, the shoes of a poor child. I asked myself why did they kill these people? Why? Let us imagine that at the time there was a small group of SS on one side, and a large group of Jewish prisoners, French and Polish, on the other. If the possibility had really existed that by eliminating those few SS men all the prisoners might be set free, who knows? If I had had a weapon, and were really sure of being able to . . . I don't know, it's very hard to say. Whatever the case, this is mere speculation, so it doesn't do much good to talk about it. I think that if you had been there, you would have sided with me.

Your Holiness, doesn't the media attention surrounding you risk altering the message you bring to us?

I don't think so. At times there are certainly sentences and words I have said which have been distorted, but in general there is a great deal of sympathy and the response has been positive.

I greatly appreciate the dedication of the press and I respect their right to stick their nose in other people's business, because I think they do it in order to expose scandals and to prevent abuse. Some people happen to be very intelligent and are experts in the art of hiding their irregular dealings. You can find this among politicians but also among businessmen and even sometimes in the religious world— perhaps even among some professors, who knows! This results from a lack of discipline on the part of those people who have an important role to play in society. The press have flair, which means they manage to uncover these kinds of situations. I think this is a very positive thing because, after all, if a person is honest, appearances should coincide with reality. A disparity between the two suggests that the person is not trustworthy, that he or she is trying to deceive others. I think what the press does is a very positive thing in this respect.

Do you think the French government is hypocritical for not having welcomed you officially, for not daring to confront the Chinese clearly on the Tibetan question?

I am not sure one should condemn a government for that. Take the example of my people: the Tibetans want more, but other people like myself, who have responsibilities, must take a great number of factors into consideration. The same thing applies to governments; they have to act in accordance with real situations. I cannot accuse an entire nation on an individual basis, but I will condemn international politics in general: I feel that something in global policy is not working at all.

Those who base themselves in an attitude of realpolitik deem that there is no room for a moral component to politics. But I think that is a grave mistake, because it is the little countries who end up suffering, and within these countries themselves it is the disadvantaged sectors that suffer most. So in the long run, because of their policies the big powerful countries also end up being roundly criticized from all sides.

I would like to relate another experience to you. I visited Moscow a couple of years ago, just after the August revolution. When I later left Europe to go back to India I met an African official who was travelling on the same plane with me. When we stopped in Delhi we chatted for a moment, and I shared with him my feelings about the recent events in Moscow. I told him that I was very glad of the fact that now that the situation between the two major nuclear powers had changed, there was no longer such a risk of nuclear war, at least for a while. I expected him to have a similar reaction. In fact it was very different.

He explained to me that before, during the Cold War, the countries of the Third World had room to maneuver and at least knew what to expect. Now that these points of reference had disappeared, they found themselves facing a period of great uncertainty. I felt great sympathy for him. I reasoned that, all the same, this Eastern totalitarian bloc had called itself "peace-loving" when in fact it used to spend an enormous portion of its budget on the manufacture of arms, and in so doing had sacrificed the happiness of its population. The Western countries, despite their faults, are fortunate to have a democratic regime which allows human creativity to be expressed fully, leading to major developments in the fields of economy, education, and science. We did, of course, witness great scientific progress in the former Soviet Union, but their achievements were often connected to military activities.

In reality the world has now become a safer place. But in the Third World, is the image of the West, in particular that of the United States, that of a champion of democracy, freedom, and human dignity? No, not at all. Why? Because of the appropriation of politics for its own sake, politicians' politics. If ethical principles were respected in foreign policy there would not be this type of problem. It is a great wrong which must be put right. I often tell my American friends: you are the superpower now, it's up to you to change this; you should return to the principles of your great statesmen like Jefferson or Lincoln, men who valued liberty and democracy, and who defended those values.

To conclude, should a politician be guided by compassion?

Yes, I think so. But an intelligent compassion, one informed by wisdom.

THE INTERNATIONAL COMMUNITY

In what ways can the tradition of Tibetan Buddhism benefit the rest of humanity?

First of all, at the heart of Tibetan Buddhism there exists a tradition of dialogue between the different spiritual branches, a tradition of dialogue which can easily be extended, I believe, to other religions. Fruitful exchanges among the various world religions and Buddhism are therefore possible. In addition, in its very essence Tibetan Buddhism ascribes fundamental importance to human kindness and compassion. These are notions which will naturally benefit the minds of all those who receive such teachings.

Unfortunately we are faced at this time with a very real danger—the total disappearance of our country and its unique cultural heritage. The Tibetans, of course, are very attached to their culture, but in Tibet they do not even have the right to express their concern for its preservation. At present it is in India, where more than 100,000 Tibetan refugees live, that we have the most advanced methods to preserve and perpetuate the Tibetan heritage in its entirety. Among the refugees there are more than 5,000 monks and scholars capable of maintaining and in turn transmitting in detail the essential teachings of Tibetan philosophy and Buddhism. There are a great number of convents designated specifically for women who wish to dedicate themselves to the monastic life.

There is obviously no doubt that the various Tibetan centers and universities throughout the world devoted to the study of Buddhism and Tibet make an important contribution to the preservation and development of knowledge about our country and its spiritual tradition. There are roughly 2,000 centers devoted to the study of Tibetan Buddhism in Europe, in North and South America, in Australia, New Zealand, and many other countries. The French people show great interest, I have noticed, in Tibetan culture. From my very first visit to your country I was struck by this and I place great hope in these ties which, since that first time, have never ceased to grow.

The truth about the history of Tibet has often been misrepresented. It is therefore essential to promulgate the true version of the facts and inform the Chinese of the truth. It will help historians and scholars to have a clear picture of the situation if the historical reality is brought to light. At the other extreme, a false, sectarian, and misleading vision will convey no positive strengths and will therefore be of no good use in working for the future. It is the power of truth—particularly at this time when more and more totalitarian regimes seem fated to disappear—which will enable us to give life once again to the cause of Tibet. Those who express erroneous and distorted opinions would seem to be hard of hearing; this is why I am reiterating my call to the so-called civilized world to take every possible measure to preserve the priceless traditions of Tibet.

Recently a great number of scientists met in Paris to express their concern over the degradation of the environment in Tibet. They suggested that the country be classified—in whole or in part—as belonging to the natural and cultural heritage of humanity. Do you think that under the present circumstances this suggestion is acceptable and that it may, eventually, be submitted for approval to the Chinese?

Yes! Aside from the fact that everything must be done to make this happen, I think that this is a very useful and perfectly feasible idea. Tibet is an ancient nation in which there are a great number of historical monuments not only of interest to Tibetans but to the entire world. Several organizations have already spoken quite seriously of preserving the Potala and other sacred sites. Some people even think that the main temple of Lhasa—the Tsuglakhang—must be protected, as well as the entire city. Why not? The capital is closely connected to the life which has evolved around the Potala. It is unfortunate that in recent years much new construction has replaced the traditional habitat, and Lhasa, whose appearance has already been completely transformed, is in danger of dying. This is yet another reason to add the capital of Tibet to the list.

What have been the consequences of the Chinese invasion to the ecological balance of Tibet, on the forests, soil, rivers, and the like? What is the present situation?

This is one of our most pressing concerns. In many regions deforestation has indeed brought about soil erosion. Moreover, this erosion is also caused by often intensive and poorly implemented mining of all the minerals our soil is so rich in; according to official Chinese documents, Tibetan soil contains 167 types of minerals, some of which are extremely rare.

But there is something even worse. It would appear that the Chinese are using an entire region of our country for the disposal of nuclear waste. It is almost certain that near Lake Kokonor there exists an entire arsenal of Chinese nuclear weapons as well as an underground nuclear research institute called the "Ninth Academy."

To all these factors contributing to the degradation of Tibet's environment must be added yet another, of great concern to many scientists in India and in the world: the pollution of the great rivers of Asia by contamination at the source—in other words, in Tibet. There is a risk that this situation will in turn affect, on an even larger scale, all the regions and countries through which these rivers run—China, Vietnam, Laos, India, Bangladesh, and Pakistan.

Will the cultural identity of Tibet be able to hold up much longer under the increasingly present authority of China?

For more than forty years of Chinese occupation the Tibetans have, despite adversity, been trying to preserve the culture which belongs to them and to which they are strongly attached. In spite of the perpetration of so much damage and destruction, it is not too late. Hope remains, not only that the culture might be preserved but also that it might be reborn. There is still threat of a great danger; I am referring to Chinese population transfers. Tibetans are actually now in the minority in their own country. In all the biggest cities in Tibet—Lhasa, Chamdo, Shigatse, Gyangtse—the population is two-thirds Chinese and only one-third Tibetan. Of course in the remote countryside one can find places inhabited solely by Tibetans. But wherever the land is more fertile or is situated at a lower altitude—offering, therefore, milder living conditions—the Chinese are settling in great numbers.

Among the documents we have received there is one dated May 1992 that mentions secret meetings held by the Chinese authorities. The purpose of these meetings, it is believed, was specifically to accelerate the population transfers from China to Tibet. What do you know about this secret document and what would its immediate consequences be for the Tibetan people?

That is correct, we have in fact received this document, which happens to be very detailed and therefore leads us to believe it is authentic.

When I was in Beijing in 1954, and in early 1955 when I was about to leave, I went to greet President Mao Zedong, Liu Shao Chi, Zhou Enlai, and other notables of the then Chinese government. Liu Shao Chi was then in some ways my hierarchical superior, because during that period I was Vice President of the Head Committee of People's Deputies. During our conversation he said: "Since you Tibetans have a vast territory and we Chinese have a very large population, it would be useful to instigate an exchange between us." That is proof of their desire, already present at that time, to undertake massive transfers of population.

Since our country was annexed by China, the number of Chinese inhabitants in Tibet has never stopped increasing from year to year, most notably in recent years under cover of a so-called "open door" economic policy. Whenever the Chinese hear of a place or a situation in Tibet that is useful to them, they settle there in great numbers with their families. Take Lhasa, for example, or the majority of Tibetan towns, where life is not as hard as elsewhere: the Chinese are now more numerous there than Tibetans, a fact Chinese officials continue to deny. In their official declarations they claim that there are roughly 10,000 Chinese in Lhasa. But the reality is totally different. It is obvious, whether to passing tourists or to Tibetans in Tibet, that there are not 10,000 but more like 100,000 Chinese presently living in Lhasa, while the Tibetan population consists of no more than 50,000. That is the situation. In certain remote regions which are nevertheless a part of the Tibetan territory, the Chinese population, even there, is greater than the native population. The effect of this situation is creating even greater anxiety among the few Tibetans remaining, as others have left to try to reach those regions where they will be in the majority. Whatever the case, the Chinese population has now reached 7 million, while there are no more than 6 million Tibetans.

Did you know that the ruling totalitarian system uses various methods, one of which consists in making public declarations which are not really applied, while other policies are energetically implemented—policies which have never even been previously announced to the public? This has been the case with the Chinese population which is increasing daily, despite official denials; this is also the case with the requirement for native Tibetans to have a permit to move around in their own country and who risk being expelled from Lhasa if they try to settle there. If the Chinese authorities are sincere in their desire not to proceed with such transfers, why do they not put an end to this tragedy? I think we have good reason to say that the Chinese government is deliberately organizing the resettlement of a Chinese population which is still expanding in their own country.

I would like to add something else. As a human being, I perceive humanity taken as a whole to constitute one single entity. These population transfers would, up to a point, be acceptable if they were carried out in a spirit of mutual understanding and respect. We would in such a case be able to consider sharing our vast country with the Chinese, who have such a high population density and who are finding it difficult to become economically self-sufficient. But from the time of the Chinese occupation, over forty years ago, this demographic aggression has been accompanied by the destruction of many sites, something which has not been compensated for by a corresponding development in the country. The last Panchen Lama himself, who was considered by all to be pro-Chinese although in reality he was not, declared in public, two days before he died, that the modest economic development brought by the Chinese could in no way compensate for the extent of the destruction that had been inflicted. The suffering endured by the Tibetans for over forty years has been immense. Of course, official Chinese documents still consider us to be a Chinese minority and call us their "brothers and sisters." They often refer to China symbolically as a great family made up of five brothers. But in this case, the elder brother never tires of tormenting the younger! I am speaking of historical fact.

The increase in the Chinese population in Tibet is naturally a source of great tension. When the number of Chinese increases in a given place, tension rises, not only because of the problems created for employment but also in other areas, such as education or health, where the effects of a Chinese majority are sorely felt. As for the money allocated for the development of Tibet, purportedly to be of help to the Tibetans in social services, education, and health, a large part of it actually ends up in the hands of the Chinese.

Other tensions are related to the environment. As you may know, bird hunting and fishing were traditionally forbidden in Tibet. In any case, Tibetans prefer to refrain from these activities. The circumambulation of holy sites, such as the Potala or the temple at Lhasa, is another source of tension. The Tibetans habitually walk around in a clockwise direction but the Chinese deliberately walk in the opposite direction. Humiliations of this kind only exacerbate the tension and increase resentment among the Tibetan populace. The Chinese government pays virtually no attention to the murder of one Tibetan by another, but the slightest hostility on the part of a Tibetan toward a Chinese is considered to be a serious crime and is consequently dealt with. There are also countless incidents of human rights violations.

The ever-increasing number of such incidents constitutes—be it consciously or unconsciously—virtual cultural genocide. I say this and repeat it whenever I have the chance. As soon as we were able to establish contact with the Chinese government, I requested, as set down in my Five-Point Peace Plan, that an immediate halt be put to population transfers. The Chinese authorities, however, have no intention of abandoning this policy, the very existence of which they deny. They claim that Tibet has never ceased to enjoy its autonomy. As you can see, this "autonomy" they speak of no longer makes any sense!

How far are you prepared to go to begin discussions with the Chinese government on Tibetan independence?

I feel that given the present circumstances it is my duty to do all I can to assure the protection and preservation of the Tibetan nation. I think the best means to this end is to negotiate with China. However, fourteen years ago when we succeeded, through the intermediary of my envoy, in establishing contact with the Chinese authorities, Deng Xiaoping placed a sizeable condition upon the negotiations. He declared that it would be possible to discuss everything except independence. Although Tibet from every point of view is an independent country, as shown by its culture, its language, and its history, the fact remains that today it is under foreign occupation.

Given Deng Xiaoping's declaration I tried on a temporary basis and in a realistic way to implement negotiations with a view to the autonomy of Tibet. I did not demand a total separation between our two countries. I told the Chinese government that the past was past, and that henceforth I would be looking to the future. We have in our possession a number of documents covering the entirety of the various records containing the report of those negotiations, and they show how hard I tried, on my side, to make a maximum number of concessions. I have the feeling that given the circumstances and the current political context, my approach is the most realistic, the only one to envision. This is what I usually call, in terms of negotiation, the Middle Way. As for any future goals, I have often repeated that it is up to the Tibetan people to decide, and the result will depend greatly on China's behavior.

In response to my Five-Point Peace Plan, in the early 1980s, the Chinese authorities suggested that I return to Tibet. I replied that the question of my return to Tibet was not the real issue, but that the goal to attain was the protection and safeguarding of the rights and culture of 6 million Tibetans. For as long as nothing has been done to resolve this problem, it is out of the question to talk of my return. If their desire to talk with the Dalai Lama concerns my return alone, all efforts will remain in vain. If, on the other hand, they wish to deal with the crux of the Tibetan question I will, for my part, always be at their disposal, whatever the place or time they suggest for a meeting. I have moreover publicly voiced two proposals in this regard.

One proposes that immediate international pressure be exerted upon the Chinese government, with an aim to beginning significant negotiations as soon as possible. My immediate task deals with this essential point.

We must not forget that the Chinese government has always considered Tibet to be an integral part of China; for this reason they feel free to do what they like with it. But from an historical point of view, such a declaration is erroneous. In 1914, when the treaty of Simla was signed, and I won't go into detail on this point, the British government recognized Tibet as an autonomous country—and this the Chinese refused to ratify. The British government would only accept Chinese suzerainty over Tibet on the condition that China respect Tibet's autonomy. The Indian government recognized Tibet as an autonomous region of China and not as an integral part of that country. According to British experts, autonomy means de facto independence. During my visit to Beijing in 1954, President Mao in person told me that at one time Tibet had been a very powerful nation, that it had even conquered China, and since we found ourselves at present to be considerably weaker, the Chinese were going to help us. He added that they would withdraw once a certain level of development had been reached. In 1956, when I was in India at the same time as Zhou Enlai, he told Prime Minister Jawaharlal Nehru that the Chinese government did not consider Tibet to be a Chinese province, but that it was a "case of its own." Whenever China has invaded other territories, no such declarations have ever been made.

Although it was drawn up under pressure, a seventeen-point agreement was signed with the Chinese. All these facts establish that it is wrong to consider, as the Chinese affirm, that Tibet has been an integral part of China since the thirteenth century. This is why I think that since the Chinese themselves consider Tibet to be a "special case," the international community should do everything possible to clarify Tibet's historical antecedents by examining them in light of international laws, and also by taking into account the differences which exist between the two cultures, Tibetan and Chinese. No one has ever asserted that Tibetan is a Chinese language. Similarly, one speaks of

Chinese Buddhism, Japanese Buddhism, and Tibetan Buddhism. In spite of this, the Chinese want to make Tibetan into a Chinese language and make our religion a Chinese religion. This does not correspond in any way to reality. International experts have declared during recent meetings that Tibet, on the basis of the right to self-determination, has the right to decide its future. This is the situation which must be made clear to everyone.

You are a spiritual leader and you are also the leader of a state which has suffered aggression for more than forty years. For someone who has met politicians from all over the world, do you ever feel a certain resentment when you see how few voices have been raised in support of your country? Do you think that Western heads of state might now be more inclined to help your country not be completely overrun by its powerful neighbor?

Tibet is indeed faced with great difficulties, but we must take into account that the country used to live in an isolation which was perhaps too extreme. It is no doubt due to our very isolation that when problems arose at the time of the Chinese invasion the newly-created situation went virtually unnoticed. Our country was subjected to an invasion and, from a certain point of view, the Tibetan question may in some ways seem like an old one. Problems which are of pressing urgency appear on the face of the planet every day. Moreover, at first glance it may seem that Tibet is not of great importance from an economic point of view.

But if you consider the general situation from a global point of view, the concern shown by people the world over for the Tibetan cause seems to me to be a very encouraging sign. In 1959 and throughout the 1960s, many countries supported our cause in the United Nations. At that time, most of them were defining their position in opposition to the Communist bloc. But I think that today the support expressed by many countries over the last few years is much more sincere, and is founded on the recognition of irrefutable fact, a delicate but real situation.

Your international activity regularly mobilizes the media, celebrities, and heads of state the world over. Does it have a real concrete effect on the Chinese position, resulting in an improvement in the situation in Tibet?

I am very happy about the interest shown by the media and, through them, by people the world over in the Tibetan cause, and I attach great importance to this interest. The fact that our cause will gain recognition in this way will, I believe, inspire the Chinese government to show greater restraint in its dealings with the Tibetan people, and to take their needs into account. One opinion holds that to oppose the Chinese or simply criticize them out of hand would not be a constructive attitude. That is not our attitude. Until two years ago the Chinese refused to consider and even rejected any declaration concerning human rights in China, on the pretext that these were their internal affairs. Gradually, however, they have been obliged to publish what is known as the "White Book" concerning human rights in their country, and driven by international pressure they have had to authorize the presence in China and Tibet of a certain number of delegations sent to verify whether human rights are being respected.

I have done everything in my power to try to set up reasonable negotiations with the Chinese government, but they have always refused. Sustained international pressure has forced them, however, to make it known, at least to the outside world, that the doors are open wide for negotiation with the Dalai Lama. Despite these efforts, the situation within Tibet has not improved much.

You speak the language of nonviolence and are very popular in the West, but do you think that what is actually happening, concretely, is enough? One gets the impression that nothing is changing in Tibet, and that there is a risk that genocide will reach the point of no return. What international political action would you advocate?

If the current situation were to carry on for ten or fifteen years, it would certainly be too late, but at present there is still a chance for success. It is for this reason that I have not stopped calling upon all nations and all governments, more and more actively. As a Buddhist I am in the habit of saying that we have three refuges: the Buddha; the Dharma, the teachings; and the Sangha, the monastic community. We can now include a fourth one: the international community. Buddha, Dharma, and Sangha are terms which may seem mysterious to you, but at the level of active support the international community becomes a fourth refuge, one we greatly need.

The moral pressure exerted on the Chinese government has opened a crack through which a voice can be heard, expressing the desire for dialogue with the Dalai Lama. Pressure of an economic nature should reinforce this moral pressure.

Would the refusal of the International Olympic Committee to assign the Olympic Games in the year 2000 to Beijing have any influence on the internal Chinese policy to allow more freedom?

In my opinion there are two ways one can view this. According to the first, the development of friendly relations with China and the increase in economic aid would encourage democratic changes. China is a very ancient nation and they deserve to host the Olympic Games. This is a totally justified point of view, but apparently it is primarily for economic reasons that the government would like to host the Olympics. The other view holds that it would be a great pity for the advocates of democracy in China, who opposed their veto to the plan, to lose heart and become demoralized. The responsibility of encouraging them by sending the appropriate signal belongs to the international community. After weighing the pros and cons I have concluded that in these conditions it would be better to postpone the idea of holding these games in China. In any case, everything has by now been decided.

Will the Chinese economic miracle give less opportunity to Tibet to regain its independence? To what extent would a degree of democratization in China be to the advantage of the West?

China's economic development should in the long run bring something positive to Tibet because the improvement in living conditions is a beneficial factor to all. It is, moreover, very important for the Chinese and for the entire world that China become more democratic, because it is the most populous country on earth. As we saw during the tragic events of Tiananmen Square, the Chinese people do hope for democracy. But where will this democracy come from? Who will inspire it?

I believe that in general the Chinese population can be divided into three categories of individuals. The first is made up of leaders and certain members of the communist party whose vital interest is to remain in power. If they feel threatened, they do not hesitate to shoot into the crowd. Students and intellectuals, who are the inspiration behind the democratic movement, make up the second category. The majority of the Chinese population constitutes the third. If world governments do concern themselves with this problem, there is a great risk that the minority presently in power will keep their power, and that the partisans of democracy will become discouraged. In a country like China, so over-populated and also armed with nuclear power, as long as the totalitarian regime we know of remains in power and continues to stockpile weapons, there is cause for grave concern. That is why it has become the entire world's responsibility to help the democratic forces both in China and elsewhere.

You were awarded the Nobel Peace Prize in 1989. Has this helped your cause?

I think the fact that I was awarded the Nobel Peace Prize certainly contributed to a greater awareness of the Tibetan cause. It is always said that it is the Dalai Lama of Tibet who was granted this distinction, never a "lama from China"!

You have been in France for three weeks, in the country where the Declaration of the Rights of Man was drawn up. What do you think of the welcome you have received from the French government? Wasn't it a bit cold?

I would like first of all to tell you how happy I am to have met the people of France; that is what is most important to me, the reason for my visit being, above all, of a spiritual nature. The conversations and exchanges I have had with the French people have been very valuable to me and very enriching. I might add that when I visit a country my position is that if the heads of government express the desire to do so, I am myself very happy to meet them, to exchange opinions and have a discussion with them. But if such a meeting might be for them a source of embarrassment, then I do not wish to meet them, in order to avoid causing any disturbance in their own country.

The creation in the French National Assembly of a study group on the Tibetan question is a very encouraging sign, proof that there is growing interest in our cause. There has also been the recent signing, by over a hundred key figures from the French artistic and scientific communities, of a manifesto containing a message of very strong support for the cause of Tibet. But we need even more support.

You continue to believe in human goodness, in human generosity. Is this conviction not somewhat old-fashioned in our times? Will it become necessary some day for your religion based on nonviolence to break with its tradition of nonviolence?

No, no, no! I firmly believe in the values of nonviolence. Recent events such as the end of the dictatorial regimes of Marcos in the Philippines and Pinochet in Chile, as well as the changes in Moscow and other countries, show quite clearly that the upheavals in the heart of the population were not a result of violence, were not caused by the use of arms, but were the result of nonviolent action. Even more recently, in Palestine and Israel, both parties met in a spirit of reconciliation after years of willfully reciprocal hatred and acts of extreme violence, and they were able to put an end to their grievances. For me, these are very positive signs in favor of nonviolence.

People realize that nonviolence is the most effective and appropriate method to resolve conflicts. To respond to violence with violence leads to problems such as what is happening in Bosnia, to endless suffering. If you could ask all those who are fully involved there the reason for their acts of violence, they would not really have a clear explanation. People find themselves involved in situations where they no longer have any control over their emotions and where there is no longer any room for logical reasoning. Do you understand? As far as I'm concerned, such a situation only reinforces my faith in nonviolence.

Your country has been occupied by the Chinese for forty years. Do you sincerely believe that the attitude of nonviolence will enable Tibet to regain its sovereignty? If so, when?

We must never forget that Tibet and China have always been neighbors and that they must remain so. For this neighborly relationship to be peaceful and harmonious in the future, it is essential that the problems dividing us at present be resolved in a nonviolent way. If we try to resolve them through violence, a feeling of resentment would remain between our two peoples, and this would make harmony difficult. Of course it takes nonviolence longer to achieve goals such as this, but I think it is the approach that will give the most positive, stable results.

The world has evolved. Democracy has been established in a number of countries—the Philippines, Chile, the former Communist bloc—and this has come about not through violence but because the people wanted it and were inspired by the spirit of nonviolence. In our case, because we have opted for a peace-loving position, many Chinese people now express sympathy for our cause and as a result are openly demonstrating their support for Tibet's struggle for independence. It is precisely for this reason that many nations are now offering more vigorous support than before. I often tell my people that having practiced nonviolence in choosing a democratic system for Tibet's future does not constitute an end in itself, but must serve as an example for the entire world. To seek peace with nonviolence is to ally intelligence and skillful means.

Isn't it true that more and more young Tibetans want to engage in armed struggle? What would you say to them?

Both in Tibet and abroad this danger exists, not only among young people but also among older people, because the Chinese government does not seem to want to understand the language of truth and justice. Of course when someone reminds me that I have been leading our struggle nonviolently for fourteen years without achieving any results, I don't have an answer to that. It is true that at times I too lose hope. In such moments I think we must call on our human intelligence, more than ever. My deep conviction remains that the nature of humanity is basically good, and that in spite of a lack of results in times past it is only through peaceful means that we will reach a solution. To give in to an attitude of violence reveals the emotions and passions that are present in our mind that have ended up dominating it. The past has shown us time and again that if we use violent means to attain our goals there will always be attendant reactions of an extremely negative nature, which are subsequently the cause of major difficulties. When passions can no longer be controlled, you end up with situations such as what is happening in Bosnia. This is why, given the causes and consequences of such an attitude, I have opted for nonviolence and will continue to do so.

You have announced that you may be the last of the Dalai Lamas. Why?

We have decided that in the future, Tibet will most certainly be a democracy. It will be up to the Tibetan people to decide the significance and scope of the office of the Dalai Lama. I have already made a completely official announcement that when I return to a free Tibet I will set up a democratic government and I will hand over all my powers. The office of the Dalai Lama will continue to exist if the Tibetan people as a whole deem it to be beneficial and desirable. It will disappear by itself if the people feel they no longer need it, and at that time the Fourteenth Dalai Lama may well be the last one. I often say, jokingly, that that is not such a bad end, because the fourteenth of the name will go down in history for not having betrayed the cause of his people.

I had the good fortune some years ago to go to Lhasa, and last year I went to Labrang and Kumbum. I was shocked and upset to see the number of Chinese who have settled in these towns over the last generation or two. What will happen to the Chinese population living in Tibet, who are now equal in number to the Tibetan population, when the country once again becomes completely autonomous and free?

Among the many Chinese who have settled in Tibet I think we must distinguish two categories of people. There are first of all those who respect Tibetan culture and traditions and who therefore can live in harmony with the Tibetan people. For them there will be no problems! However, there are a great many immigrants who have nothing but scorn for Tibetan traditions and they are in perpetual conflict with our culture. For them, cohabitation will be uneasy, and for us as well!

How can you not feel hatred against those who seek to annihilate you?

From a Buddhist point of view, it is very important to understand the link which exists between the one who is causing harm and his victims. In reality, what is a person doing when, in a spirit of malevolence, he harms others through his destructive, negative acts? According to the Buddhist view, that person is preparing to endure great suffering and torment in the future as a karmic result of his malevolent acts. However, the one who suffers from others' evildoing and misfortunes is using up the karmic results of his past negative acts. He is purifying his karma, but while he is in the process of using up his past karma through suffering, he is not accumulating any new negative impressions. Consequently, far from considering the person who harms us as an enemy or an object of hatred, if we understand what suffering awaits him in the future he becomes for us a rather special object of compassion. To think in this way can be of great help.

I am going to give you a concrete example. In India I recently met up with a man I had known long ago, the abbot of a monastery who spent twenty years of his life in prison and in labor camps in Tibet. While we were speaking together he declared to me that during the entire time of his imprisonment in Chinese jails the greatest danger he had encountered was that of losing his compassion for the Chinese. I found his attitude most remarkable.

If we look at the current situation in Tibet, and the relations between Tibetans and Chinese, the Tibetans are the oppressed and the Chinese are the oppressors. Up to now the Chinese have been successful in their work of oppression, and their desire for conquest has been fulfilled; they should be happy. But, in fact, the Tibetans for the most part seem much happier than their oppressors. This is yet another persuasive reason for fostering compassion for the Chinese, rather than hatred.

Can a democracy, like the one you envision for Tibet, do without an army and a system of defense?

Good relations between India and China—the two most populous countries on the planet—are essential, both to guarantee peace in the world and in this particular part of the world. As Tibet no longer plays its traditional role as a buffer between those two countries, whose armed forces sit entrenched facing each other, the situation has changed dramatically and the tensions are increasing. My goal, therefore, is to make Tibet, whatever its future political status, into a peace zone, denuclearized and demilitarized, which would once again, by virtue of its strategic position, become the peace-keeping buffer zone for the entire region. The two neighboring countries would without doubt reap great benefits from this. It would not, in any case, be a unique example in the world—Costa Rica has been a prosperous country for forty years, entirely demilitarized, and their standard of living is higher than that of their neighbors for the simple reason that unlike their neighbors they do not need to add great military expenditure to their national budget. Wherever I go I always say that demilitarization is not a problem exclusive to Tibet. It is a problem which must be dealt with on a global scale.

Secondly, Tibetan culture and its distinct religion, both founded on the nonviolence that I call Buddhist culture, have been the bearers of peace of mind and serenity wherever they have spread, in the south, in the Himalayan region, in the north and the northeast of Inner and Outer Mongolia, and even in regions which were once part of the former Soviet Union. Moreover, in many places in China itself one can still find Tibetan-style monasteries and temples, which shows to what extent the influence of our culture spread throughout this entire Asian region. Tibetan culture can even be a help to the Chinese; after all, Buddhism is not foreign to their spirit. That is why the survival of the Tibetan culture and people in that part of the world must be of particular interest to the Chinese.

It is therefore altogether useful, important, and justified that the Tibetan nation survive, not only from a moral point of view, but also from a practical perspective.

HUMAN RIGHTS
A MEETING WITH AMNESTY INTERNATIONAL

I have great admiration for all those who work in the field of human rights. I feel that your activism does not seek solely to protect the rights of the individual, but also contributes indirectly to the progress of humanity as a whole. Generally, people who criticize established governments and politicians have a more long-term vision, and they are the first victims of the systems they criticize. I think that in fact your work to protect the rights of these individuals affects the nation in question as a whole.

Although the Communist authoritarian system of the former Soviet Union was very harmful, I believe that the present Chinese system is even worse. For example, the regime in the Soviet Union allowed notables like Pasternak or Sakharov to emerge; such a thing is unthinkable in China. If the slightest movement is felt it is immediately crushed! Thus, although many horrible things happened in the Soviet Union, the democratic movement was effective. Unfortunately, this is not the case in China. Therefore, those visionaries who love freedom and fight for democracy are very important for their country.

Clearly, human rights are a universal value; it is out of the question to begin to make distinctions on the basis of culture, education, or any other characteristic, because by birth every human being has the same rights. For cultural and historical reasons some countries have been shown to discriminate on the basis of sex, or, in particular, ethnic or social traits. Such systems are backward and they must change. The system that advocates universality and equality is the most evolved; it is therefore up to the backward systems to adapt and evolve toward something more modern, and not the opposite.

I would again like to express my gratitude toward your organization which has worked tirelessly for Tibet. You have done a great deal and I thank you. I think that if the prisoners who stagnate and are tortured in prisons and labor camps in Tibet were present today, they would thank you from deep within their hearts. On this occasion I do so, in their name.

WORDS OF TRUTH

PRAYER BY HIS HOLINESS THE FOURTEENTH DALAI LAMA

O Buddhas, Bodhisattvas, and disciples
Of the past, present, and future
Who possess such remarkable qualities
As vast as the ocean,
And who hold all helpless and sensitive beings
As if they were your only child,
I pray to you to consider the justice of my cry of anguish.

All of Buddha's teachings dissolve the suffering
Of cyclic existence and of a peace turned only toward oneself;
May those teachings spread and propagate prosperity and happiness
Throughout this vast world!
O Keepers of the Dharma, scholars and realized practitioners,
May your ten practices of infinite virtues be sovereign!

Humble, sensitive beings are tormented relentlessly
By suffering,
Completely dominated by their negative actions
Which seem interminable and most intense.
May all their fears arising from unbearable war,
From famine and sickness, be appeased
So that they might breathe freely in an ocean of happiness and
    well-being!
And in particular, pious beings
From the Land of Snows who, by different means,
Are massacred mercilessly by hordes of barbarians
Belonging to the dark side,
Make known, for the sake of goodness, the power of your
    compassion
So that most rapidly this river of blood and tears may cease to flow!

Those who, pitilessly cruel, objects of compassion,
Are alienated by demonic emotions
Who with light hearts destroy themselves and others,
May they realize the eye of wisdom
Knowing what is to be done and what is to be abandoned
And abide in the glory of friendship and love!

May this wish from the deepest heart for the total freedom of all
    Tibet,
Awaited so long,
Come about spontaneously.
Grant us soon, I pray you, the chance to savor
The happy celebration of spiritual and temporal power joined!
O Protector Chenrezig, with compassion take care
Of those who have endured a thousand trials,
Sacrificing with fortitude their most precious lives,
Their bodies, their riches,
For the good of the teachings, the believers,
The people, and the nation!

Thus the Protector Chenrezig made great appeals
In the presence of the Buddhas and Bodhisattvas,
To embrace in full the cause of the Land of Snows.
May the favorable results of these prayers henceforth appear
    promptly!
Through the profound interdependence and emptiness
And relative forms
United with the power of great compassion
Of the Three Jewels and their Words of Truth,
And by the power
Of the infallible law of cause and effect,
May this truthful prayer come to pass
Rapidly, without impediment.

PART IV

BEYOND DOGMA

HARMONIZING ACTS AND WORDS

Your Holiness, what advice might you give those of us who are working to develop Buddhist communities and organizations in the West?

As I often tell my Buddhist friends, if we want to keep the excellent tradition of Buddhism developed in Tibet alive, it will depend on the existence of freedom in Tibet. To that end, since you are already working together, I would like you to continue to work for the cause of Tibet's freedom with those who are already doing so.

We try to make a distinction between the words "freedom" and "independence." The use of the word independence is somewhat delicate. Obviously, I have been trying to establish contacts with the Chinese government and begin serious negotiations. For fourteen years I have been trying my best, persisting in this approach, and pursuing my efforts incessantly to bring these negotiations to a successful conclusion through direct talks with the Chinese government.

I would like to share some of my thoughts with all of you gathered here, brothers and sisters in Buddhism. First of all, Buddhism corresponds to a new tradition, a religion which did not previously exist in the West. Consequently, it is normal that all those who are interested in Buddhism in its Tibetan form would also like to be informed about and continue to study other religions and traditions. This is perfectly natural. However, for those who are seriously thinking of converting to Buddhism, that is, of changing your religion, it is very important to take every precaution. This must not be done lightly. Indeed, if one converts without having thought about it in a mature way, this often creates difficulties and leads to great inner confusion. I would therefore advise all who would like to convert to

Buddhism to think carefully before doing so.

Second, when an individual is convinced that Buddhist teachings are better adapted to his or her disposition, that they are more effective, it is quite right that this religion be chosen. However, human nature being what it is, after their conversion and in order to justify it, such a person may have a tendency to want to criticize his or her original religion. This must be avoided at all costs. Even if the previous religion does not seem as effective as he or she would have liked (and this is the reason for the change), this is not sufficient reason to claim that the old religion is ineffective for the human spirit. That religion continues to bring immense good to millions of people. For this reason, as Buddhists, we must respect the rights of others, for other religions help millions of people. In particular, we are in the process of trying to create and maintain a perfect harmony among all religions. In these circumstances it is absolutely essential to be aware of the need to respect other religions.

Third, in the Tibetan Buddhist tradition emphasis is always placed on the combination of study and practice. Of course, it may happen that you devote yourself more or less to study. Some people may pursue their studies very far, others may be satisfied with a more limited level of study. Whatever the case, at the foundation you must never separate study, reflection, and meditation. You must also preserve the tradition of practice in which study, reflection, and meditation are indivisible.

Fourth, I would like to insist upon the importance of non-sectarianism. It sometimes happens that people attribute an exaggerated importance to one or another of the different schools and different traditions within Buddhism, and this can lead to an accumulation of extremely negative acts with regard to the Dharma. The advantage of non-sectarianism is that after receiving the transmission of the instructions, initiations, and explanations pertinent to each different tradition, we will be able to have a better understanding of the different teachings. From my own experience, this is without doubt very beneficial. Consequently, if we keep a non-sectarian attitude, as we receive teachings from different traditions, think about them, and put them in practice, it is certain we will improve our understanding of the Dharma. This is why non-sectarianism is so important.

Traditionally in Tibet there have been two approaches used by the many great scholars and accomplished masters. Indeed, while some concentrated on the study and practice of their own tradition, their own spiritual heritage, others expanded the field of their study and their practice of Buddhism from a non-sectarian point of view. This tradition already existed in Tibet among the great masters, and I think that today this non-sectarianism is extremely important and is the best Tibetan custom to follow.

There is a fifth point I would like to go into. For just under thirty years, Tibetan Buddhism has been spreading through the different continents of our earth. Lamas, tulkus, and geshes have made an enormous contribution to the flowering of Tibetan Buddhism all over the world, aided by hundreds of thousands of students and disciples. During the same period, some rather unhealthy situations have arisen, and this has led to difficulties. Initially this was due to an excess of blind faith on the part of the disciples and also to certain teachers who eventually took advantage of their disciples' weaknesses. There have been scandals, financial and sexual abuses. Such things happen! As a result I must insist at this point that it is absolute necessary that both disciples and teachers keep the goal in mind—to preserve a perfectly pure Dharma. It is the responsibility of us all to put an end to this type of unhealthy activity.

The Buddha taught the four ways to bring together the disciples, and this was to ensure the welfare of others. The six perfections (Sanskrit: *paramita*) are practiced to achieve one's own good, and the four ways of bringing together the disciples to achieve the good of others. This involves, first of all, giving material gifts, then practicing right speech, then providing help, and finally harmonizing one's words and acts. Above all, it is important to keep this last point in mind. If we do not master our own mind, it is impossible to master the minds of others. We do not know whether or not it is possible to master the mind of another, but it is what we are supposed to do! Whatever the case, it is essential for those who claim they wish to help others that they control their own minds. To do this it is very important nowadays for teachers to be reminded again and again of the teachings of Buddha on how to help others and harmonize words and acts.

As far as the disciple is concerned, to quote a Tibetan proverb: A disciple must not throw himself upon a spiritual master "as a dog throws itself upon a piece of meat." A disciple must not rush to place their trust immediately in a master, but must rather take the time to reflect carefully and examine the master's qualities before establishing a spiritual bond with them by receiving their teachings. It is preferable to receive the teachings of a master while viewing him or her first and foremost as a spiritual friend. We must not rush to hear their teachings and consider them our master at the same time. Little by little, if having observed them we are convinced that they are a true master, fully qualified and worthy of trust, we can follow their teachings by considering them our master. We must not hurry.

The sixth point which I would like to go into regarding Dharma centers concerns our oft-invoked prayer: "May all beings find happiness and its causes." This is something we should apply directly by doing something useful for society, engaging in social activity in the community, by trying to help those who are in difficulty, such as those with mental or other problems, for example. This does not necessarily mean we should teach them the Dharma, but rather use the teachings ourselves in order to help them. I think such activity directed toward others is something we should develop. It is the natural conclusion of another common prayer: "May all beings attain happiness and be free from suffering." On this principle, if we can bring good, even if only to one person, we are fulfilling in part the vow we have made. Moreover, the entire Buddhist community of these centers should participate in social engagement by assisting others, and I think this is something very important with regard to the operation of these centers.

A vegetarian diet is not obligatory for Buddhists. Still, for those of us who follow the teachings of the Great Vehicle, it is important. But the teachings of the Buddha were open and flexible on this subject, and each practitioner has the choice to be vegetarian or not.

Large gatherings are sometimes held in Dharma centers and when there are such festivities, celebrations, or teachings, I think that if a great number of people are to be fed it is very important to serve only vegetarian food for the entire duration of the meeting.

Seventh point: we often say this prayer, "May the teachings of the Buddha (the Dharma) be propagated." If Tibet regains its freedom, this will certainly help to preserve the vast and profound teachings of Buddha, including the Lesser and Great Vehicles as well as all the Tantras. There is therefore an obvious connection between the freedom of Tibet and the preservation of the teachings of Buddha in the world. If this were not the case, if the fundamental question of Tibet's freedom were solely a political issue, then as a monk and a disciple of the Buddha's tradition I would have no reason for such concern. But the two aspects are closely linked.

Even when I am advocating the demilitarization of Tibet, that it be made into a peace zone, although the term "demilitarization" is not strictly speaking a term from the Dharma, the project is nevertheless closely related to the Dharma. Many of you, representatives and members of the different centers, are among those who have already contributed to the cause of Tibet's freedom. I thank you for that and ask you to continue your efforts, bearing in mind the relation between the preservation of the teachings and the freedom of Tibet, in order to give practical expression to the vow that the Buddha's teachings be preserved and developed.

My last point—you must keep your mind happy and know how to laugh!

AN INTUITION COMMON
TO DIFFERENT RELIGIONS
THE DALAI LAMA'S VISIT TO THE GRANDE CHARTREUSE

When you describe my visit to the Grande Chartreuse in the newspapers, I hope you will emphasize the importance I attach to the harmony which must be created and preserved among all the religions.

144 · BEYOND DOGMA

I still believe that the great spiritual traditions all share the same message of love, compassion, and forgiveness. They also have the potential to serve humanity and contribute to the reduction of tension and conflict among people. I think these common elements form the most solid base upon which to build harmony among religions and to formulate a common message: that of practicing with the aim of increasing our personal mastery and thereby transforming and improving our own lives.

For many years, whenever I encounter practitioners—and I emphasize the meaning of this word—I feel that, due to their practice and their extensive knowledge of the great values of the religion they practice, they can easily understand the values of others; for this reason they have a natural ability to establish understanding and harmony. You know, as I do, that in the past there have been many tragedies related to religion throughout the world, and even today, in Africa, in Bosnia. Despite these tragic events I think that the cooperation among religions is improving daily. Access to our religion of choice, like being able to eat according to our hunger, is a right that I have always defended. We eat good food in order to have a healthy body, and the more varied it is, the better! The same thing applies to religion, the food of the human spirit. As mental dispositions and characteristics vary from one individual to another, it is preferable to have a choice among several religions. Each one has its own essence, its specific qualities, and its unique potential, and this is an excellent thing. From a broader point of view, all religions have points in common, and on this basis we can work together.

When I heard that in this region there are monks and nuns who live cloistered and devote their entire life to religion, I wanted very much to meet them. As soon as I went into the courtyard of the monastery I was overwhelmed by the silence and beauty that emanated from that place, the great peace and strong spiritual vibrations. It was also quite cold there! I shared my thoughts with those I met, particularly regarding the similarities between our spiritual experiences and the contemplative life of our respective traditions. While talking with the prior I discovered that the very strict daily program of prayers followed by these monks, who have taken the vow of poverty, presented a number of similarities with the practice of Buddhist nuns and monks.

What is astonishing is that these similarities do exist and did not derive from any exchanges that might have taken place long ago. We have been separated for over a millennium, and yet there seems to be something like a supreme influence, or let us say rather, an intuition, common to our respective traditions. I feel I have had an extraordinary, very satisfying experience, one which moved me a great deal.

RELIGION FOR HAPPINESS

There are five billion inhabitants on earth among whom we can, I believe, distinguish three categories. First, about a third have faith in a religion, a spiritual path; at the other extreme, a second third reject religion as mental poison and feel nothing but disdain for it; and finally, a last third are indifferent, neither for nor against religion.

The human beings who make up these three categories equally wish to be delivered from suffering and to find happiness. In this respect there are no differences between them—all humans try their hardest to find a way to obtain satisfaction and happiness and to avoid suffering. Let us make a comparison between those who accept religion, who have faith in a spiritual path, and those who reject it outright. We might wonder who has a happier, more satisfied mind—those who have a religion, or those who reject it? One difference becomes evident when people are confronted with difficult circumstances. Those who are without any spiritual approach find that their minds immediately lapse into anger and, upset as they are, they have nothing with which to combat their difficulties. Those, however, who do have a spiritual support find their confidence reinforced and are therefore better equipped to deal with their problems serenely.

If you compare rich and poor people, it often seems that the people who have nothing are in fact those with the least worries. As for the rich, while some wealthy people know how to use their wealth intelligently, others do not, and we can see to what degree they are constantly anxious and tormented, torn between hope and doubt, even if they seem to have been successful in everything. It is certain that a spiritual path, a religion, is extremely beneficial and useful when we have difficulties that go beyond our everyday capabilities. I often tell my friends that if it came to pass that those who rejected any spiritual tradition were perfectly happy, we should also reject religion, because by practicing it we are in fact searching for happiness and satisfaction.

There are two major categories among the great world religions. Some conceive of a Creator, while others place more emphasis on the transformation of the mind. If we can transform and master our mind, that is what we call nirvana. If, on the other hand, we are incapable of controlling it, we are slaves to our mind, and this is samsara. Those are the two main divisions. I think that all beings have different aspirations, and that the diversity of religions is therefore perfectly good and desirable.

Buddhism, the Jain religion, and a part of the Samkhya philosophy, a Hindu tradition, are among the traditions which do not conceive of a Creator. Nonviolent behavior, not harming others, and the view of interdependence are the two main aspects characterizing the essence of the Buddhist religion.

How shall we define nonviolence? In the best sense it means not only not being violent, but also bringing good to others. If that is not possible, then at least we must absolutely avoid causing harm to others.

How can we put this nonviolence into practice, and how can we find this happiness we are all looking for? These goals depend upon a number of causes and conditions, the essence of which is that our ability to master, train, and transform our mind will lead us to satisfaction and happiness, while our inability to bring about this transformation will always lead to more suffering. We must act in such a way so that our aspirations, which are common to all beings—the pursuit of happiness and the avoidance of suffering—will not be contradicted by the result of our actions. We must of course use as our support everything which will lead us to this goal.

When we seek to describe to a beginner the structure of the path to enlightenment, we speak of the five paths and the ten stages (Sanskrit: *bhumi*). Gradually, progressing along these paths will lead to the omniscience of Buddhahood. We also speak of the three *kaya:* the *Dharmakaya,* or Truth Body; the *Sambhogakaya,* or Enjoyment Body; and the *Nirmanakaya,* or Emanation Body. The last two—the Sambhogakaya and the Nirmanakaya—emerge from the space of the knowledge of the Dharmakaya, the absolute plane, symbolized by the primordial Buddha, Samantabhadra, whose blue color is the sign of his immutability. We bathe here in the light of Samantabhadra, whose feminine aspect is Samantabhadri. Samantabhadra represents the primordial aspect linked to great joy, and Samantabhadri the aspect of primordial purity, the counterpart of Samantabhadra.

When we speak of Samantabhadra and Samantabhadri, we do not consider them to be creator gods. It is from their space of knowledge and gnosis that samsara and nirvana became manifest and appeared.

Of course it is important to know the different stages of progress on the spiritual path, but it is also essential to know how to act in everyday life. The Kadampa masters said that some people may look like practitioners of the Dharma when they have a full stomach and are comfortably seated in the warmth of the sun, but that they completely lose this aspect when, upset by difficult circumstances, they become angry and quarrel. That is what we must not do. It is therefore very important to put the teachings of the Dharma into practice every day, day after day.

What are the cardinal virtues we must cultivate in our daily practice? First of all, kindness, a good heart, patience, tolerance; also, knowing how to be content with little, simplicity—all of these points are shared by all religions.

In the Buddhist way in particular, how do we go about accomplishing our goal of contentment and satisfaction? To explain this, we will have to think about the law of cause and effect, the law of karma, the state of dissatisfaction which is found in samsara, and also how to transform our happiness and take upon ourselves the suffering of others. Hatred and malice are the greatest dangers to peace and happiness. In order to prevent hatred and anger from taking root in ourselves, we must first of all avoid discontent, for it is the root of hatred and malice. To do this we must work to keep our minds serene, relaxed, and open. Once hatred is expressed with all its strength and power, it is very difficult to find an antidote to it. It is very important, therefore, to prevent and impede anything which can give rise to hatred.

Animosity, aggression, and hatred are mainly produced by discontent, and to prevent this dissatisfaction from taking hold we must keep our mind in a state of serenity, openness, and vastness, always at ease with itself. Indeed, if our mind is narrow and closed in upon itself, the slightest thing will be a source of irritation and discontent, and we will be extremely vulnerable to dissatisfaction, and consequently to anger and animosity. It is therefore very important to maintain balance, openness, and serenity in our state of mind. Our happiness is closely tied to that of others. It is fundamentally dependent on all those around us. We must always be aware of this and when we are happy and satisfied we must recognize our debt of gratitude for the kindness of all beings.

It may happen, in this life, that we will meet enemies, people who wish to or who do harm us. But the essence of the Buddhist way, in particular that of the Great Vehicle, the Mahayana, is kindness, compassion, and bodhichitta, the mind of enlightenment. If anger and hatred arise in us, the strength of our kindness and our spirit of enlightenment must be able to resist them. It is therefore indispensable to be able to show patience. The Way of the Bodhisattva cannot do without this mastery of patience. If we think about it, how can patience best be practiced and developed? Patience needs the support of an enemy—indeed, we will not need to exercise patience toward a Buddha, a master, or a spiritual friend. Indeed, it is due only to those who wish to harm us, those we call "enemies," that we will be truly able to cultivate and develop patience. An enemy gives us a unique opportunity to practice patience and thus to develop all the qualities of the Way of the Bodhisattva. Instead of considering our enemy as something undesirable, we must on the contrary treat him with respect, with gratitude, for he gives us this unique chance to practice the Way of the Bodhisattva.

If we prove our kindness and altruism, we will obtain both courage and certainty; with each passing day our life will be happier, more serene, and satisfied. In this regard, although I personally do not have much experience of this, I try to make the most of the little patience that I have.

We will never cease progressing and realizing a more perfect happiness if we can practice in this way, day after day, month after month, year after year, life after life.

What can the Dharma offer to the West?

In the West, whether to our brothers and sisters, Christian monks and nuns, or to lay practitioners, Buddhism can bring the help needed to develop even more love and compassion, qualities which are at the heart of all religions. It can also help to improve concentration in contemplation.

How can spirituality and worldliness be in harmony?

With regard to secular acts, we talk mainly about the the eight worldly considerations: the idea of importance we attach to joy and suffering, to gain and loss, to fame and obscurity, and to praise and criticism. These eight worldly considerations have different degrees, and can, for example, be entirely negative, mixed, or extremely positive. In the most extreme case, the mind of one preoccupied by worldly life will be constantly preoccupied with hatred, or with the desire to possess something to the detriment of others, or even with deceiving others. In such a case we are, of course, very far from a spiritual quest. Nevertheless, in the case of a worldly act inspired by noble sentiments, for instance, if the attitude or intentions of a person involved in running the economy of a country or a place are inspired by kindness or concern for the welfare of others, it is then a simple matter to integrate the spiritual with the secular.

UNIVERSAL RESPONSIBILITY
A VISIT TO LOURDES

I am particularly happy to come today to this place of pilgrimage, now a center for believers because it has been blessed. Our message today, addressed to all beings thanks to this meeting of all religions and people, is a message of universal peace and love. I am therefore very happy to have this opportunity for all of us to pray together in this holy place. I thank you for having made this possible and for welcoming me here today.

We have been reminded here of the unspeakable horrors of war, for example, the town of Sarajevo, where many innocent people have perished or continue to suffer. We must bear this in mind. Such tragedies clearly show how difficult it is to appease our passions, which once unleashed seem to have no true deep reason, and how difficult it is to find a solution when emotions have become uncontrollable. Of course human intelligence enables us to distinguish between a temporary benefit and an ultimate benefit, but this ability to judge is nevertheless eclipsed by the force of emotions when passions invade our mind.

This is why I think that inner peace, inner disarmament, is essential, and must absolutely not be neglected. It will be difficult to attain a durable, practical world peace if we do not make peace in our own minds. I also believe that education, the media, and politicians should constantly emphasize this aspect of human thought: to make peace within in order to make peace on the outside. Of course, if our minds are driven by aggression, malice, and envy, latent aggressiveness cannot fail to be expressed as soon as external circumstances seem to warrant it.

I think this meeting today has great significance. Indeed, there is no doubt that all religions share the values of kindness, love for others, and the spirit of tolerance. It is on this basis that we must establish harmony. It has become extremely urgent, given the present state of the world, to emphasize harmony and greater understanding between human beings and religious representatives. But it must be clear that kindness, brotherly love, and tolerance are not virtues reserved only for those who believe. These are fundamental virtues for all human beings.

This visit today gives me two causes for hope. On the one hand, the fact that representatives of all religions are gathered here in this Christian holy place to pray together will, I hope, contribute to the discovery by all human beings of the need to develop inner peace. I also trust that our meeting will lead to greater understanding and mutual respect. This may be a major source of inspiration for all beings, so that they might develop greater serenity and peace within themselves by realizing the harmony that reigns among us. I therefore ask that all beings follow the example of these representatives of the different religions and develop this sense of responsibility and of the necessity of achieving harmony.

Your Holiness, in your opinion, are there universal values shared by all religions which can help build lasting peace?

I believe that not only are there values shared by all religions, but also by all human beings and all forms of life. Love of one's neighbor, affection, tenderness, kindness are all at the basis of a universal ethic, and I think that every being, animal or human, knows how to appreciate affection when it is given. So what is the role of religion? The role of religion is to give the means to reinforce and develop even further the natural kindness of sentient beings.

I think society can live in peace thanks to the inner peace human beings have developed through their intelligence. Thus, I believe that to have world peace we must first have inner peace. Those who are naturally serene, at peace with themselves, will be open toward others. I think this is where the very foundation of universal peace lies.

All religions have the methods and spiritual techniques to further develop this inner disarmament, this inner peace. We must understand each other and work in harmony with one another, because it is our responsibility to develop in human beings their natural disposition for peace.

Just as one often asks a doctor if the day will come when there will no longer be any disease, do you think that after dozens or hundreds of meetings like this one, the day will come when the world will truly be at peace?

I do believe and continue to hope that we can attain universal peace on earth. But, of course, there will always be minor problems here and there.

Your Holiness, you have just visited a Catholic shrine. Do you hope to one day go to Jerusalem or Mecca?

I am particularly happy to have gone today, in person, to the shrine at Lourdes, the heart of this holy place of pilgrimage I had heard of in the past. I was deeply moved.

Of course I have been attending services and taking part in inter-religious exchanges for a long time. For two years I have been planning to do a major pilgrimage to holy places in the company of representatives of other religions. When we visit such places we benefit from their atmosphere, we pray together, or we may simply meditate and commune with our thoughts in silence. I have already done this in India and am happy to begin again today. I believe these sites awaken in us a feeling of communion and understanding much greater and deeper than a simple intellectual comprehension. I would like very much to begin such a pilgrimage by visiting Jerusalem and Mecca, but I do not know when circumstances will allow me to go there.

Have you and the other representatives discussed among yourselves the issues raised by conversion, changing from one religion to another, in particular the different forms of Protestantism, Catholicism, or even Buddhism here in France?

In our private meeting, a Christian quoted to me an inscription of King Ashoka, which speaks of how intolerance towards other religions can destroy one's own religion; how the prosperity of a religion is linked to respect for other religions.

What do you think of the work of solidarity taking place between Christians in the West and in China?

Christians have always been a minority in China, and they have suffered as such. Moreover, the lack of communication due to the political regime has certainly limited their vision of the international situation. I think, therefore, that any dialogue that can be established with Christians outside China can help them to open their minds to the realities of the world.

THE LIBERATION OF ALL BEINGS

You have said that according to Buddhist philosophy there is no Creator, no God of creation, and this may initially put off many people who believe in a divine principle. Can you explain the difference between the Vajrayana Primordial Buddha and a Creator God?

I understand the Primordial Buddha, also known as Buddha Samantabhadra, to be the ultimate reality, the realm of the Dharmakaya—the space of emptiness—where all phenomena, pure and impure, are dissolved. This is the explanation taught by the Sutras and Tantras. However, in the context of your question, the tantric tradition is the only one which explains the Dharmakaya in terms of inherent clear light, the essential nature of the mind; this would seem to imply that all phenomena, samsara and nirvana, arise from this clear and luminous source. Even the New School of Translation came to the conclusion that the "state of rest" of a practitioner of the Great Yoga—Great Yoga implies here the state of the practitioner who has reached a stage in meditation where the most subtle experience of clear light has been realized—that for as long as the practitioner remains in this ultimate sphere he or she remains totally free of any sort of veil obscuring the mind, and is immersed in a state of great bliss.

We can say, therefore, that this ultimate source, clear light, is close to the notion of a Creator, since all phenomena, whether they belong to samsara or nirvana, originate therein. But we must be careful in speaking of this source, we must not be led into error. I do not mean that there exists somewhere, there, a sort of collective clear light, analogous to the non-Buddhist concept of Brahma as a substratum. We must not be inclined to deify this luminous space. We must understand that when we speak of ultimate or inherent clear light, we are speaking on an individual level.

Likewise, when we speak of karma as the cause of the universe we eliminate the notion of a unique entity called karma existing totally independently. Rather, collective karmic impressions, accumulated individually, are at the origin of the creation of a world. When, in the tantric context, we say that all worlds appear out of clear light, we do not visualize this source as a unique entity, but as the ultimate clear light of each being. We can also, on the basis of its pure essence, understand this clear light to be the Primordial Buddha. All the stages which make up the life of each living being—death, the intermediate state, and rebirth—represent nothing more than the various manifestations of the potential of clear light. It is both the most subtle consciousness and energy. The more clear light loses its subtlety, the more your experiences take shape.

In this way, death and the intermediate state are moments where the gross manifestations emanating from clear light are reabsorbed. At death we return to that original source, and from there a slightly more gross state emerges to form the intermediate state preceding rebirth. At the stage of rebirth, clear light is apparent in a physical incarnation. At death we return to this source. And so on. The ability to recognize subtle clear light, also called the Primordial Buddha, is equivalent to realizing nirvana, whereas ignorance of the nature of clear light leaves us to wander in the different realms of samsaric existence.

This is how I understand the concept of the Primordial Buddha. It would be a grave error to conceive of it as an independent and autonomous existence from beginningless time. If we had to accept the idea of an independent creator, the explanations given in the

Pramanavartika, the "Compendium of Valid Knowledge" written by Dharmakirti, and in the ninth chapter of the text by Shantideva, which completely refutes the existence per se of all phenomena, would be negated. This, in turn, would refute the notion of the Primordial Buddha. The Buddhist point of view does not accept the validity of affirmations which do not stand up to logical examination. If a sutra describes the Primordial Buddha as an autonomous entity, we must be able to interpret this assertion without taking it literally. We call this type of sutra an "interpretable" sutra.

Do you think it is possible to be both Christian and Buddhist at the same time?

I just replied to this question indirectly when I said that belief in a Creator could be associated with the understanding of emptiness. I believe it is possible to progress along a spiritual path and reconcile Christianity with Buddhism. But once a certain degree of realization has been reached, a choice between the two paths will become necessary. I recently gave a series of teachings in the United States and one of these teachings was about patience and tolerance. At the end there was a ceremony for taking the Bodhisattva Vows. A Christian priest who was in the audience wanted to take these vows. I asked him if he had the right to, and he replied that yes, of course, he could take these vows and still remain a Christian.

Christ's words "Love thy neighbor" embody for us the Christian religion. What is your message to humanity when you meet another human being?

Love of one's neighbor, kindness, and compassion—these are, I believe, the essential and universal elements preached by all religions. In spite of divergent philosophical views, we can establish harmony among all spiritual traditions on the basis of these common traits of love, kindness, and forgiveness. I always insist on this point and devote a great deal of energy to it. Most difficulties between religions come about because of people who, having failed to transform and bring peace to their own minds, do not really apply their own beliefs yet try all the while to impose them on others. This unfortunate behavior can provoke serious conflicts, although I have noticed a considerable reconciliation between the different religions, more particularly between Tibetan Buddhism and Christianity. We have actually set up a very constructive program of exchanges between monks and nuns of our two traditions.

Christianity is in a state of crisis in the West. What advice do you have for Christians who are in doubt?

My personal experience leads me to say that we must concentrate on the essence of our tradition rather than become attached to ritual and ceremony. The ritual and ceremonial aspects are, of course, linked to the changing customs of a place and an era. However, the essence of religion, of which teachings on the fundamental suffering of humankind are a part, is very useful.

What is the usefulness of dialogue between Buddhists and people of Judeo-Christian views?

As I have already said, despite differing philosophical views, great religions do have a common point: all seek the good of humanity. The numerous exchanges we have already had underline the common points which, through this dialogue, have enabled us to enrich our understanding of respective spiritual practices. I was particularly happy to note great similarities on the level of the contemplative life and practice. Another thing which has made a great impression on me is the way in which the representatives of the Christian tradition are continually striving through social involvement—charity and aid— to improve the well-being of society and its members. There are also such people among Buddhists, but not as many. What Christians are doing from a practical point of view to help others is an example for us all. We cannot deny how in the past, present, and, no doubt, future, the Christian community has and will always turn to help humankind by trying to relieve suffering and bring about well-being.

All human beings have greatly varied dispositions and characteristics. It is therefore advantageous, even desirable, to have many spiritual paths to cater to the diverse needs of diverse people. I often try to understand how certain so-called fundamentalist or extremist movements have come about. Upon reflection, I think that instead of concerning themselves with their own spiritual evolution, these fundamentalist movements fall into extreme attitudes by imposing their religion on others. Having failed to achieve their own maturity—the basic purpose of every spiritual tradition is, after all, the transformation and mastery of the mind—they impose on others a transformation that they themselves have not yet achieved, a constraint which is at the root of hatred, attachment, and all sorts of negative passions. These are often the signs of fundamentalism.

On the other hand I think we naturally feel great respect for all the other forms of spirituality if we practice our religion in a perfectly pure fashion, with the understanding that in an initial stage the purpose is our own transformation. I also think that dialogue, communication, and exchange with other traditions are essential factors for mutual understanding. If the representatives of the different religions remain isolated, insular, they can have only a very fragmented and partial vision of other spiritual traditions, and misunderstandings will remain. Exchange, contact, and shared personal experience can only lead to greater mutual respect.

Do you think that the teachings of Buddha and those of Christ are different in their essence and, if so, what do you see as the major difference?

There are numerous convergences and differences between the two teachings. Among the differences is the philosophical view of the Madhyamika, the Middle Way, which refutes all forms of substantial, inherent reality, and which seems difficult to reconcile with the essential teachings of Christianity. However, some of my Christian friends have expressed the sincere desire to take the Bodhisattva Vows; I just spoke of an example of this. Since there do exist bodhisattvas endowed with extraordinary courage and universal vision, whose extremely beneficial behavior is generated by a profoundly altruistic mind which excludes no living being, I gave them my approval, even though their philosophy contradicts that of the Middle Way. I told them, therefore, that they could take these vows and still remain Christian.

Let us take the example of a bodhisattva following the Vaibhashika school, the Particularists, whose aspiration to realize perfect enlightenment for the good of all is authentic. Even if a person's philosophical view of what truly constitutes Buddhahood is incomplete, and prevents him or her from fully attaining this omniscient state, that person is nevertheless a sincere and altruistic bodhisattva. The Vaibhashika point of view conceives of nirvana as liberation from cyclic existence—that which is realized by an arhat—which, as it is not complete according to the Madhyamika school, is not equivalent to that of a fully realized Buddha.

Can one follow a spiritual path without religion, consider Buddhism as a kind of healthy lifestyle?

The decision to follow a particular religion or not is first and foremost an individual one. If you do not follow any religion whatsoever, and do not therefore take into consideration beliefs with regard to future lives, it is nonetheless of crucial importance to be a person who shows warmth, a good heart, and altruism. In this way, not only will you yourself know greater happiness and joy, but you will also become a more productive and beneficial member of the society in which you live, more positive and helpful. In this case you will gather and enjoy the fruit of your positive, virtuous acts in your next life, even if in this life you have paid no attention to the notion of future life, since you don't believe in it.

I sometimes hear people say, "I am a believer, but I do not practice." Is such an attitude possible with regard to the teachings of the Dharma?

Of course. Many people are in this situation, even Tibetans! A faith that is not practiced is superficial, conditioned by the social climate and customs of the country. When we can deepen and strengthen our faith, a sort of emotional link will be created; it is that link which inspires us and urges us to become sincerely committed. The worst case is that of a person who, while he has his faith in the teachings, understands them only to a certain degree and doesn't integrate them. His mind consequently remains undisciplined and is not transformed in the slightest way.

Do you think that the formality of religious rituals makes it harder for us to understand emptiness? Wouldn't ordinary people find simplicity in the form of the rituals to be more beneficial to their enlightenment?

Let us take the example of Milarepa, who performed few rituals but meditated deeply on emptiness, and who shows us that a commitment to rites and ceremonies is not necessary to reach the highest realization. Nevertheless, these rituals do have significance. They were taught by Vajradhara, the mystic, tantric form of Shakyamuni Buddha. I do not mean by this that he indicated how many times one must strike the drum or how one should play the cymbals. Rituals vary according to context and circumstances; some are performed to accompany a dying person, others to dispel interferences, etc. What is important is that they be performed in the spirit of enlightenment, bodhichitta, and if not with complete realization of emptiness, at least with a certain understanding of it. Once these preliminary conditions have been met, such rituals will surely be of great benefit.

I would like to attain a certain level of realization, but given the considerable amount of time—three endless eons, it is said, to realize enlightenment—such a wish now seems totally presumptuous.

It is necessary to train one's mind in a spiritual path. The time spent in cyclic existence, in the grasp of ignorance and karma, is so much greater than the "three eons" devoted to spiritual practice. As for the future, if we do not take the initiative to commit ourselves to an authentic path we will continue to remain under the yoke of ignorance and karma in our future lives for an infinite period of time— immense in comparison to the three eons we are talking about.

If we begin now to put into practice the teachings of our chosen way, with the goal of reaching perfect enlightenment some day, however long it might take, isn't this worth it? We wouldn't waste or lose a single day, contrary to what we have been doing since beginningless time. It is unthinkable for us to continue to spoil this and future existences for centuries without end, when we know how to recognize the very precious nature of each day that we devote to spiritual evolution.

Is it possible to realize great compassion without having realized emptiness?

The answer to this question has been given in the Buddhist text, "The Ornament of the Mahayana Sutras" by Maitreya, which refers to two sequential stages of the path. The first concerns the practitioner of superior ability who first realizes emptiness, an accomplishment which leads to the development of great compassion and bodhichitta, enlightened mind. The second shows another possible chronology, in which realizing great compassion and bodhichitta precedes a realization of emptiness.

I don't have a clear understanding of the relation between emptiness and compassion.

We have just seen that the relation between emptiness and compassion can be interpreted according to the order of their realization. A certain experience of emptiness is also developed simultaneously with the understanding that false illusions and ignorance can be stopped and eliminated. Once you have recognized the possibility of liberation from ignorance and suffering, obviously your attitude toward suffering will be very different. On the other hand, if there is no recognition of the perspective of liberation, just thinking about suffering can become a negative and morbid pastime, of little use and to no end.

As for knowing how compassion will increase our understanding of emptiness, I am certain that the more your compassion increases in intensity, the more you will try to find the cause of suffering. You will seek to find out whether suffering has a cause and how it is produced. Then there will be an investigation of the actual origin of suffering. When, for example, you meditate on your own suffering, you look for its cause. This in turn raises the following question: will it be possible to eradicate the roots of this suffering? This is where meditations on emptiness begin to play a part.

We have already pointed out that certain people, like the Vaibhashika bodhisattvas, can bring about great compassion without actually fully realizing emptiness. Although this school of thought presents only an incomplete view of emptiness, the bodhisattvas who share this view have developed immense compassion. It may also happen that in a very intense state of compassion there will be no understanding of emptiness, and that, conversely, compassion will not appear even if you are absorbed in a state of realizing emptiness. Why is this? Because these two states of mind are very different in terms of cognitive faculties. In the situations which normally follow the realization of emptiness—when, for example, you are in touch with events or phenomena which seem to be illusions—your perception of the human being is also like an illusion, and on this basis, there is, undeniably, the possibility to generate powerful compassion for human beings.

This is why Buddhist texts speak of different levels of compassion. There is compassion directed toward living beings which does not take into consideration their true nature, which, among other things, is impermanent and has no self. The second type is reinforced by the understanding of the impermanent nature of your object of compassion. A third level is enhanced, or rather induced by, the consciousness that living beings, although they are devoid of inherent, independent existence, cling to a form of inherent and independent existence, and are bound therefore to cyclic existence. This last form of compassion is said to be devoid of object. And finally there is great compassion, unlimited and sufficiently powerful to generate what is known as the uncommon attitude of bodhichitta, that extraordinary state of mind which takes on the responsibility to lead all beings to happiness.

Some scholars maintain that even the arhats, the shravakabuddhas, and the pratyekabuddhas are endowed with this great compassion, which is still not, in such cases, powerful enough to produce great determination, that exceptional attitude that enables one to work incessantly for the good of all humankind. Only the mind of a bodhisattva has developed that type of compassion, the power of which leads to bodhichitta, the aspiration to realize perfect enlightenment for the salvation of all beings. The texts refer, therefore, to different types of enlightenment. Do not forget that the compassion felt by whoever seeks to protect sentient beings from all kinds of suffering is different from that which motivates the aspiration to liberate them all from suffering.

Some say that the Gelugpa school is the purest of the four Tibetan lineages, and that the Nyingmapa school is not Buddhist. I have heard that you received teachings from the Nyingmapa school. This puzzles me greatly. When you follow a certain tradition, can you receive instruction from another?

The four traditions of Buddhism in its Tibetan form all follow the same master, Shakyamuni Buddha. But the chronological order in which the teachings evolved and the essential points on which the schools insist have delimited certain differences. In spite of this, they are all guardians of Buddhist tradition and its essence, whether they derive from the Hinayana, the Mahayana, or the Tantrayana.

In Tibet itself there used to be two types of masters. The first were those who were dedicated to a non-sectarian approach and put into practice the instruction handed down by the four main schools. The second type were those who concentrated on one particular lineage and paid almost no attention to the others. My temperament inclines me to the non-sectarian approach, an ecumenical path which I admire, as much on a level of my own affective attraction to it as for the benefits derived. One of these benefits, of which I have had personal practical experience, is that each of these four schools presents and explains its teachings in its own way, placing emphasis on particular aspects of the doctrine.

If one acquires global knowledge of the diverse interpretations of the path and of the practices, one comes to realize that they are mutually enriching, that the understanding of one school improves the knowledge of the point of view presented by another. Take the Tantra of Guyasamaja, where there is the question of the four voids; my knowledge of Dzogchen helps me to understand them. And, in turn, my knowledge of the four voids explained in the Tantra clarifies and enhances my understanding of Dzogchen. These mutual contributions are therefore very beneficial, not only on the level of inner enrichment but also because if we practice the four main tendencies we do not risk accumulating the non-virtuous marks which derive from critical and sectarian attitudes toward the other schools. I also think it serves as a fine example of harmony.

As for the Nyingmapa school, one of the characteristics informing the depth of its approach is the practice of the Dzogchen, the Great Perfection. At the heart of the Sakyapa school we also find unique, clear, and penetrating qualities, in its presentation of the *Lamdre*, "The Way and Its Fruits," and more particularly in the *Lobche*, "The Traditions of Instructions." The explanations of the inseparability of samsara and nirvana which it gives are absolutely remarkable, particularly where anything to do with the view of non-apprehension is concerned, that element of depth and clarity which gives this approach its unique quality. The presentation of the Mahamudra by the Kagyupa school insists greatly upon the practice of clear light, as in the practice of the Six Yogas of Naropa. As for the Gelugpa school, Lama Tsongkhapa explains a view of emptiness shared by the Sutras and Tantras. His presentation of emptiness in relation to interdependent origination has never been equaled, which makes it, too, unique.

The terminology used in the texts very closely follows that adopted by the Indian masters, in their writings collected in the *Tengyur,* all of their treatises translated into Tibetan. The ultimate approach of the Dzogchen talks of "cutting through," the Kagyupa and the Sakyapa of the "unity of depth and clarity," and the practices of the Gelugpa school address the "indivisible unity of bliss and emptiness." All arrive, ultimately, at the same point; this is what I have found through my personal experience and my reflection. Of course, everyone is free to have their own commentary. One also finds differing approaches and presentations within a same school, be it the Gelugpa or the Nyingmapa. This is perfectly normal, perfectly natural.

Take the example of Sakyapa master Tsarchen Losel Gyatso, founder of the Tsarpa monastery, whose two principal and closest disciples studied with the same master, but their presentation, comprehension, interpretation, approach, and style were different. In the same way, the Kagyupa school, which includes four main divisions and eight minor subdivisions, professes varied approaches and interpretations. It also happens that many masters present their own tradition as being the supreme teaching.

You ask that we reflect on the nature of suffering and the origin of afflicting emotions. It seems that this comes primarily from subtle attachments to duality, which creates the separation between oneself and others. Is this subtle duality inherent in the mind, or is it acquired as a result of habitual, instinctive tendencies? Should we uproot it or transform it into a purer form?

When we use words such as "inborn" or "instinctive," we must envision two interpretations. For example, one of the inborn qualities inseparable from the mind is its fundamentally pure nature. Such qualities are inherent in the mind. Moreover, the potential we have to realize the omniscience of a Buddha and realize the ten powers is not only inherent in the mind but also inseparable from its essential nature.

Another understanding of the word "inborn" is in terms of origin, where it signifies that we are incapable of affirming at what exact moment this or that quality was acquired. I am referring here to those faculties which have not been developed intellectually or brought about through any form of conditioning. Let us also consider negative impulses—our erroneous perceptions, our afflicting emotions, and our disturbing thoughts—whose impressions or potential have been in our flow of consciousness since beginningless time; this is something that concerns all sentient beings living in cyclic existence, human beings as wells as birds, insects, etc. These impulses are said to be inborn, instinctive, but also adventitious—not in a sense where they might have been acquired at a precise date in one of our lives, but rather that they are ultimately separable from the fundamental nature of the mind. They have no effect upon the nature of the mind itself, nor do they abide there. This is why they can be detached from the mind.

To speak of dualistic appearances is also to imply various interpretations. One relates to the apprehension of the two truths—conventional or relative truth, and ultimate truth—as two distinct entities. Even the scholars of the Gelugpa tradition have diverging opinions on this subject. Some claim that mental defilements of this ignorant apprehension are manifest and conscious, others claim that it is a more unconscious dualistic apprehension. The impulses for such a dualistic mind exist; they are called the veils of knowledge. Another understanding of this dualistic apprehension refers to the apprehension of phenomena and events as if they had inherent, independent, and objective existence. This form of dualism is on an even more gross level; it is in fact the very root of cyclic existence.

So we have different levels of duality. The first, which I just mentioned, although we cannot say it is at the origin of cyclic existence, is in fact much deeper than that: it is still rooted in our consciousness, for even those who are liberated from the bonds of samsara still have subtle dualistic impulses, veils to omniscience. Shantideva's *Bodhicharyavatara* explains that the ignorant mind which apprehends an independent existence is considered to be like an afflictive veil, meaning that it is at the origin of samsaric suffering. For an individual to be liberated, he or she must root out and eliminate this ignorance.

Can attachment to dogma be a hindrance to ultimate liberation?

The answer to this question differs according to one's point of view. Does it reflect a general point of view, or more specifically a Buddhist approach? In the latter case, attachment to the concept of emptiness is a fairly dangerous obstacle, not to mention the attachment one might have for the doctrine.

Could you go into more detail regarding attachment to emptiness and tell us what ignorance it reflects?

This form of attachment, which consists in taking emptiness to be an absolute entity, is a view which we qualify as irreparable and incurable. The Buddha explained in the Sutras that digestive problems are resolved if you take the appropriate medicine, and if you do not, then the medicine becomes a problem instead of a solution.

If it is necessary to find a spiritual guide in order to progress along the path, what criteria will enable us to determine whether the guide is a good one?

The qualifications of an authentic Buddhist master are described in the Vinaya as well as in the Sutras and Tantras. The first criterion is that he be a scholar or at least be familiar with what he is teaching. Lama Tsongkhapa said that whoever wishes to find a guide must also become familiar with the necessary qualities before looking for them in a master. Whoever wishes to teach and have disciples must therefore accept students who are familiar with the qualifications sought in a master. Once they recognize that he has developed those qualities they will be able to qualify him as a master.

You said that trust between the spiritual guide and the disciple is necessary. When this mutual trust has been lost and the disciple is no longer in touch with his or her guide, what advice could you give so that he or she may continue to progress on the path?

The wisest thing is to stop thinking about this problem and maintain a neutral attitude in your dealings with the spiritual guide in whom the trust and faith have been lost.

Is it necessary in order to progress along the path to have a spiritual guide close by? Or can you, for example, have as your guide His Holiness the Dalai Lama, who lives in India?

I think that in the beginning it is much wiser to take the teachings as a guide. The physical person matters little at this stage of one's involvement on the path. As you progress, all the while acquiring a certain experience, you will need spiritual advice given by a qualified person. But be cautious in your choice, examine him carefully and make sure of his qualities, to avoid the difficult and distressing situation of having placed your confidence in a individual who might lie to you, deceive you, or even cause you harm. Many authentic masters who contribute a great deal to the Dharma can now be found among those who teach Tibetan Buddhism. Although those who serve the Dharma are still small in number, it is essential to be able to distinguish between those masters who are truly upright and sincere from those who dishonor the teachings of the Buddha.

How can we continue without our master when he is gone?

The *Bodhicharyavatara* certifies that one can continue to receive the blessings of Buddhas after they have left their bodies. If your master should die, you can of course find among the living lamas one who will be best suited to you, and follow him. If this is not possible, continue to remain connected with your lama, for you will still be able to receive his blessing even after his death. When conditions are ripe and circumstances are favorable, it is possible for us to meet our master in dreams or visions and to receive his teachings during mystical experiences.

What might be the benefit, for ourselves or others, in withdrawing from the world on a retreat, whether short or long?

The benefits of a retreat are to be found in your isolation from distraction. On a retreat the main goal is to isolate your mind from distractions, and this is why we refrain from having contact with other people and, more importantly, from the casual talk that could result from that contact. If one strays from the essential goal of the retreat, locking yourself away in the solitude of a hermitage will serve no purpose. The Christian monks who live sincerely in this state of mind have impressed me greatly. I was told, on a recent visit to the monastery of the Grande Chartreuse, that their tradition was over a thousand years old. I was able to talk with them and I noticed that although there had been no communication between Tibet and the outside world for centuries, there were striking similarities between our respective ascetic lifestyles. These encounters left a great impression on me.

Is there a reason to become a Buddhist monk or nun in the West, where the structures needed to support them in their studies and monastic life are nonexistent? Isn't it more difficult after having taken vows than to remain a lay follower?

If you really think about it, the best defense is built where your enemies are! To be able to observe your vows and at the same time resist the worldly temptations of an environment where so many circumstances tend to awaken one's desires—is this not admirable, marvelous behavior? The true practitioner of the Dharma does not feel the need to be isolated from the society he or she belongs to, any more than the person who is only interested in personal well-being and happiness. In our era it is preferable to remain an integrated member of society.

As a rule, it seems to be easier and more practical to lead a secular life in the West, while at the same time devoting yourself to spiritual practice. Do not ever be too eager to become ordained as a monk or a nun. Such eagerness excludes you from society and may even induce some people, on the pretext of leading a religious life, to become some sort of magician dressed in exotic costumes.

Bear in mind, however, that when we say that monastic life is the root of instruction, this refers mainly to the doctrine of the Vinaya which deals with the ethics of monastic discipline. If the choice of a monastic life were of no importance, why would Shakyamuni Buddha, our master, have chosen it?

What is the difference between meditation and concentration?

Concentration is an aspect of meditation. I do not know the exact connotations of the Western term "meditation," but in Tibetan we use the word *gom,* the etymology of which is "to familiarize one's mind with the object"—that is, you familiarize yourself with the object of your meditation, from one session to the next, time and again.

Meditation involves several aspects. You aim to accustom your mind to qualities such as love and faith. You unite your mind with the object of your meditation, for example, compassion, in such a way that your mind becomes compassionate. Likewise, where faith is concerned, when you meditate you create stability for your faith. And so we might say that love, faith, or compassion infuse your mind with their positive qualities. The object of your meditation inspires your mind, and puts it, so to speak, under its influence.

Then again, if we meditate on impermanence, emptiness, etc., the objects of meditation are, in this case, objects of apprehension upon which you fix your attention. Not only meditations on the remarkable qualities of the mind but also those devoted to the nature of reality may be of two types: analytical meditation and non-analytical concentration on one point. Another form of meditation is that which we call mental calm: this is one-pointed concentration, meditative absorption; whereas meditation of penetrating insight belongs to the category of analytical meditation.

As for meditations on the deities, they enter into the category of visualizations, a practice where one takes on the aspect of the chosen divinity. Through imagination, you identify with the deity, eliminating at the same time the concepts and referents of your ordinary reality. However, in the highest class of Tantras, the penetrating view has transcended any analytical process to enter the stage of contemplative absorption. Meditations on emptiness in the context of Mahamudra and Dzogchen are also of this type.

The human body is presented in the eighth chapter of the Bodhicharya-vatara *as a repository for filth. Isn't this vision linked with a Hinayana concept, while in the Vajrayana the body is perceived to be fundamentally pure? How can we reconcile the two approaches?*

In the Buddhist approach that I teach, I often refer to the "Four Hundred Stanzas" of Aryadeva, a text dealing with the Middle Way. The first stage along this spiritual path explains that you must refrain from any negative act. When you put an ethic like this into practice, disciplined as it is by the abandonment of what we call the ten non-virtuous acts, a life spent conforming with the fundamental moral precepts will result in a higher rebirth, as a human being, for example. One of the aims of your practice, therefore, is to obtain a favorable rebirth. At this stage of the path, this type of rebirth is lauded and presented as a worthwhile goal.

The next stage of your progression requires that you meditate at length on non-self. This is the principal antidote to ignorance and all the disturbances of the mind that ignorance creates. You wish to eliminate all the afflicting emotions, as well as any impression obscuring the mind; that is, you seek to liberate yourself from cyclic existence and thus to realize nirvana, the cessation of all illusions, of all suffering. This determination—to free oneself from the bonds of samsara—is founded on very pronounced renunciation. It is here that meditations on the impurities of the body take place. The higher rebirths presented to you as a desirable and honorable prospect are henceforth considered to be states which must be abandoned, because they are still part of cyclic existence. Your goal has evolved; it has been transformed from that of obtaining better, more favorable lives into a desire to be free of cyclic existence altogether. The goal now is Buddhahood.

At the third stage, that of the Tantras, the perception of the body changes radically, since, in the meditation on yourself as the deity, all ordinary appearances, including those of your human body, are dissolved into emptiness. The essence of your mind comes forward out of this empty space in the form of a divine body. The usual perception of your body has been extinguished in emptiness; you are now the divinity with a pure form, which in no way contradicts the stage where your body, eager for renunciation, was seen in its ordinary aspect—its impure aspect, in other words.

In the context of the higher Tantras, the body is considered to be a very precious means for rapidly attaining enlightenment. Although the practitioner is fully conscious of the imperfections and impurities of the components of the body, which Shantideva has described, this does not blind him. He knows that impurity, imperfection, and impermanence exist, but he also knows the marvelous potential within himself. He knows he can direct it appropriately toward a superior goal, thanks to the higher Tantras where various techniques serve to preserve and even increase vitality and physical energy. Such a vision renders the body extremely precious—not that it can be said to be pure, perfect, and desirable as such, but because the tantric practitioner knows how to distinguish between the gross and subtle levels of consciousness and is henceforth capable of implementing different methods—meditations on the psychic channels, the drops, and the energies—in order to quickly attain his goal: Buddhahood. As the channels, drops, and energies are subtle physiological constituents of our human body, the body is in this case seen from a very positive angle.

Tantric practitioners also use negative emotions to progress along the path. This is not to imply that anger, attachment, or jealousy, among others, are healthy, good, and desirable—far from it. The point is in fact to use the subtle energy underlying the strength of each of these emotions, to channel it into our practice and use it toward a positive goal. We have an analogy to explain this specific aspect of the Tantras: just as insects who are born in the stump of a tree grow by devouring the stump until it is totally destroyed, the meditative state produced by the use of the energy of emotions consumes them totally. The forms of the deities and of their mandalas are many, and it would take too long to explain them here. The symbolism of all these aspects—all together—corresponds each time to a particular goal or context.

The impurity of a woman's body is often mentioned in the Bodhicharyavatara. *How can this be explained and what is the position of Buddhism in regard to women?*

The passages in Shantideva's text which you mentioned refer to teachings transmitted to a group of fully ordained monks. It is therefore to their attention that Shantideva describes the impurities of woman's body. But if the practitioner is a woman, her contemplations will take into account the repulsive aspects of the male body. The purpose—to eliminate carnal desire—is the same. Aside from the fact that men cannot carry children in a womb for nine months, their bodies are similar in terms of purity and impurity.

As for the status of women in Buddhism, it is necessary to make a number of clarifications here. The tradition of the Vinaya, the monastic discipline, mentions seven types of precepts, the highest of which is the full ordination of bhikshus and bhikshunis. At the level of ordination the opportunities are identical for men and women, but the ancient tradition has maintained a hierarchy in which monks are considered superior to nuns. For example, a fully ordained woman, even if she has taken her vows before a monk, must sit behind him. The Mulasarvastavada tradition holds that a woman must receive full vows from a congregation made up of both bhikshus and bhikshunis, whereas a man may receive them from a gathering of bhikshus only.

After distinctions of a hierarchical order come those related to gender. It is said in the Vehicle of the Bodhisattva, as well as in the first three classes of Tantras, that it is necessary to have a male body to attain full enlightenment. Nevertheless, the highest class of Tantras, the fourth, insists quite specifically on the attitude that a man must have toward a woman—that he must never scorn her or look down on her, among other things. Conscious attention is drawn to this in particular. Moreover, these higher Tantras completely accept the fact that one can realize enlightenment in one's lifetime in a woman's body. Even if the practitioner is a fully ordained monk, the requirement specific to the practices of this class of Tantras is to bow down before the women one encounters and to walk around them, although such conduct is not required of women practitioners of this class of Tantra if they encounter a man.

You here have proof of the very important position allocated to women, which may provoke certain reactions. I think discrimination toward women developed in the monastic tradition reflects a certain social system prevalent at the time of the Buddha. As the social environment has evolved, I think that it is now time to consider necessary changes and alterations. It is with this in mind that I have suggested convening a meeting to bring together the various representatives of monastic communities, in order to examine the possibilities for reform.

It does happen that two vows may contradict each other. In this case, the superior vow has ascendancy, as when a vow from the Vinaya conflicts with a Tantric vow. A fully ordained monk, for example, cannot, according to monastic discipline, touch precious metals or hold money; whereas the Bodhisattva Vows say that you are transgressing one of the precepts if you refuse gifts offered to you in a spirit of compassion, trust, and faith. That is an example of conflict between two vows. The response is to consider the higher vow as having precedence over the lower one in the hierarchy of precepts. The Bodhisattva Vows say you must put in your pocket what is given to you! To refuse to do so is a transgression of this class of vows. The attitude of the bodhisattva therefore takes precedence over the monastic vows.

It is true that as a rule there are only Tibetan men to be found on the dais where I generally give teachings, but I think this is a kind of discrimination which, fundamentally, is of little importance.

The Dharma essentially reflects a practice of the mind. Are spiritual practices which place emphasis on the body, such as hatha yoga, false paths?

I am not very familiar with the ins and outs of hatha yoga. Its goal is certainly positive because if the body is healthy, the mind will also find a certain equilibrium. One can say that it is therefore a profitable physical exercise. In tantric practices, where the emphasis is placed primarily on the experience of subtle clear light, numerous and varied physical exercises are executed, particularly in using the constituent elements of the body.

What are the ten virtuous acts spoken of in Buddhism?

Three concern the body: one must not kill, steal, or engage in sexual misconduct. Four others are verbal: do not lie, defame others, speak offensive words, or engage in frivolous conversation, which relates to everything that might be said under the influence of afflicting emotions. Finally, the last three virtuous acts are of a mental nature: do not develop covetousness or malice and, finally, do not hold false or perverted views, such as the extreme view, close to nihilism, which totally denies spiritual perfection.

What we mean by "erroneous views" generally includes absolutist, eternalist, and nihilistic views. But in the context of the ten virtuous acts, only nihilistic views are implicated. It is therefore on the basis of a lifestyle disciplined by ethics that one abstains from committing the contrary acts, the ten non-virtuous acts. When faced with a situation where you might possibly commit such negative acts, you abstain from committing them. A life rooted in ethics has at its foundation the abandonment of the ten non-virtues in favor of the practice of their opposites.

If we have committed a serious negative act, how can we let go of the feeling of guilt that may follow?

In such situations, where there is a danger of feeling guilty and therefore depressed, the Buddhist point of view advises adopting certain ways of thinking and behaving which will enable you to recover your self-confidence. A Buddhist may reflect on the nature of the mind of a Buddha, on its essential purity, and in what way disturbing thoughts and their subsequent emotions are of an entirely different nature. Because such disturbing emotions are adventitious, they can be eliminated. To think of the immense well of potential hidden deep within our being, to understand that the nature of the mind is fundamental purity and kindness and to meditate on its luminosity, will enable you to develop self-confidence and courage.

The Buddha says in the Sutras that fully enlightened and omniscient beings, whom we consider to be superior, did not spring from the bowels of the earth, nor did they fall from the sky; they are the result of spiritual purification. Such beings were once as troubled as we are now, with the same weaknesses and flaws of ordinary beings. Shakyamuni Buddha himself, prior to his enlightenment, lived in other incarnations that were far more difficult than our present lives. To recognize, in all its majesty, our own potential for spiritual perfection is an antidote to guilt, disgust, and hopelessness. Nagarjuna says in "The Precious Garland of Advice for the King" that pessimism and depression never help in finding a good solution to any problem. On the other hand, arrogance is just as negative. But to present as an antidote to it a posture of extreme humility may tend to foster a lack of self-confidence and open the door to depression and discouragement. We would only go from one extreme to the other.

I would like to point out that to set out on a retreat for three years full of hope and expectations, thinking that without the slightest difficulty you will come out of it fully enlightened, can turn into a disaster, unless you undertake it with the most serious intentions. If you overestimate your expectations and have too much self-confidence, you will be headed for dissatisfaction and disillusionment. When you think of what the Buddha said—that perfect enlightenment is the result of spiritual purification and an accumulation of virtues and wisdom for eons and eons—it is certain that courage and perseverance will arise to accompany you on the path.

At what moment between death and rebirth do you lose awareness of your earlier existence?

The memory is more or less clear, depending on the individual. Some people, in their earliest childhood, are able to remember events from their past life. But as soon as a child is traumatized by something, the greater the shock of that trauma, the stronger its impression will be on the child's mind. When I was two years old, there were no toilets in our house. One day as I went outside to obey the call of nature, I saw an enormous camel coming toward me. I was so terrified by this vision that I took to my heels. I do not recall very well whether I ran off right in the middle of this natural physical act, but because the experience was very intense I still have very clear and precise images of this event.

The same thing applies to anything which has left a very strong mark on a person's mind. If our memory is very developed we can remember events from a former life. It would also appear that in our early childhood, although our sensory faculties are only in a developmental stage, we have greater ease in remembering a former existence. This is comparable to what happens in nature: as it rained yesterday, the mildew in the earth is fresher today, but under the sun it will disappear eventually. The older we get, the more we collect new experiences in our lives and the more the marks of past existences become blurred. What could be more normal than such a process! But when the clear light of the process of death arises, the appearances and perceptions of the life we are about to leave fade away in order to cease completely. As for the intermediate state that follows death, depending on our karma we will have visions corresponding to our next existence. Those whose memory is exceptional can, in certain cases, perfectly remember events lived hundreds of lives before.

How can we make the fear of death disappear, together with the destructive or suicidal temptations that may be connected with it?

To deny suffering and avoid thinking of it is not a very effective means of overcoming it. A much more effective method is to face the problem head on and analyze it from every angle. In other words, confront it. The same applies to death, a natural stage of our existence. Death is part of life. To become familiar with its process helps us to become used to the idea of death. Once this is done, when death arrives you will neither be shocked by its arrival nor frightened by its unexpected aspects. This is true whether one is a believer, practicing Buddhism or not, practicing daily or not. A number of factors change our reactions on approaching death. Whether we overcome the fear and anguish which ordinarily accompany the experience of death will depend on the methods we apply during our lifetime.

What is the outer sign of death? How can you ascertain whether a person is indeed dead?

The most genuine method, moreover very difficult, is based on the examination of the respiratory process. The Scriptures mention different exterior signs that announce that death is imminent. A certain quality of sadness is one sign. During the actual process of death, external physical signs accompany the reabsorption of the constituent elements of the body.

What is the most beneficial way to help someone who is dying?

Whether that person follows a spiritual path or not, the most important thing is to try to help him or her die with a serene mind and to make certain nothing will come to trouble his or her mind during this critical phase. To further ensure such a climate of peace, the best thing is to surround the dying person with an atmosphere of love and tenderness, as much as possible. This is the reason why it is sad, tragic in the extreme, to abandon someone at the time of his death and leave him deprived of any affection or help.

You mentioned compassion and the understanding of emptiness as ways to ease suffering. How can we transmit this message to our patients, many of whom are elderly?

If they are people who believe in a Creator God, followers of Christianity, Judaism, or Islam, it seems to me it would be easier to explain to them that what they are going through is in accordance with a divine plan. As for the person who professes no religious beliefs, he must accept that death is a natural event, a normal episode in life, and that it is not imposed upon him alone but concerns all beings, without exception, at one time or another in their existence. Be aware, however, that I cannot give you answers which might be too general for specific individual cases. I think we must adjust our sensitivity to the history of each individual and in this way find the most appropriate way to help that person.

PART V

INTERDEPENDENCE
AND EMPTINESS

INTERDEPENDENCE:
SCIENCE, NATURE, AND CONSCIOUSNESS

Albert Einstein, the father of the theory of relativity, once remarked: "I determine the authentic worth of a man according to one rule alone: to what degree and with what purpose a man has freed himself from his ego." Your Holiness, to what extent does this rule seem to you to apply to the teachings of the Buddha, and constitute a preface to any fruitful dialogue between human beings?

At the heart of Buddhism and in particular at the heart of the Great Vehicle (the Mahayana), great importance is placed on analytical reasoning. This view holds that we should not accept a teaching of the Buddha if we were to find any flaw or inconsistency in the reasoning of that teaching. It is advisable, therefore, to adopt a skeptical attitude and retain a critical mind, even with regard to the Buddha's own words. Does he himself not say, in the following verse, "O Bhikshu, as gold is tested by rubbing, cutting, and melting, accept my word only on analysis and not simply out of respect." It is important to follow this advice. In such a context I see no problem in having a discussion with my scientific friends and I am always extremely interested in doing so.

To get down to the actual question, when we speak of the "apprehension of self," we must recognize different levels of this apprehension. I generally distinguish between two ways of thinking about the ego. The first, the thought of "I" which naturally springs to mind, is not only correct but also necessary. For example, to feel courage, we must have confidence in ourselves. To have great self-confidence, we must believe in our abilities and strengths, and to do this we must have a very strong idea of our self and our ego. This thought is therefore positive and constructive.

The other way of thinking of "me," "I," can lead to contempt for others. This is the apprehension of self based on a vision of ourselves transcending reality, a false perception which cannot be dissipated simply by prayer. We must reflect and meditate on the non-self of the individual, on the fact that all phenomena are empty, devoid of independent existence. The false apprehension of self grows weaker as the mind gradually becomes used to the view of the non-self of the individual.

All the ancient Eastern philosophies devote an important place to the analysis of the agent-self. According to ancient non-Buddhist Indian philosophies, there exists a self called *atman* which is separate and different from the aggregates. According to Buddhist texts, on the other hand, there is no self that is different from the aggregates or separate from them. That is why we speak of the non-self, *anatman*. The existence of a permanent, single, independent self, different from the aggregates, is refuted. However, the existence of an agent-self is not refuted. The ego which exists, the conventional self, is designated on the basis of the aggregates. All systems of Buddhist philosophy agree in recognizing the existence of the ego in relation to the aggregates, but not all interpret the nature of the ego in the same manner.

First of all, one Buddhist philosophical school affirms that each of the five aggregates which make up a sentient being is the self. Another school posits that the ego is the aggregate of consciousness. A third affirms that the ego is what we call the innermost consciousness, or "storehouse consciousness" (Sanskrit: *alayavijnana*). According to one of the views of the Madhyamika-Prasangika school, the ego surely exists in relation to the aggregates, but we would not be able to find it among them. It is affirmed that the ego exists simply as a label or simple designation on the basis of the five aggregates which make up the individual. When we use the expression "simple designation," this does not mean that the ego simply does not exist, but eliminates the notion that the ego exists by virtue of its own nature. There exists, nonetheless, an imputed self which is dependent.

And here we meet up with what Einstein said: according to Buddhist tradition, great importance is given to the absence of an absolute existence of the ego, for it is indeed thanks to the understanding of the non-self that we can weaken the various and very powerful mental factors, such as pride and jealousy, with which we are afflicted. In Buddhism not only does the individual entity exist, it progresses from the ordinary state of being into Buddhahood. Does this reply correspond to what you expected?

Yes, it does.

If you do not understand my answer to a question, I can go on until it is clearer. And if that it is still not clear, I will persevere to make it even clearer!

You have professed your interest in dialogue with scientists, regarding science in general, and technological progress. Buddhism has taken root in Western countries that are strongly shaped by science and technology. Are you simply eager to obtain information or adapt to our culture, or do you think that modern science and Buddhist spirituality may have a reciprocal impact, that scientific process may be associated with a spiritual quest?

From my own experience and the discussions and contacts I have had with the scientific community, I have noted that there is room for exchange in certain fields, in particular cosmology, neurobiology, particle physics, and psychology. On the one hand, I think that the way in which Buddhist texts treat these different disciplines can without doubt offer a new approach in the study of these sciences. In addition, I believe that the great development through science of experimental technical studies and their results can bring many things to Buddhists themselves. Both will certainly enjoy great mutual benefits.

Whether this remains on the level of acquisition of information or leads to a more personal application will depend on each individual. I would even venture to say, without talking about science, that for some people the teachings of Buddhism do not go beyond the level of information and are therefore not implemented. Yet believers are reminded that everything we perceive is a teaching. In any case, the global approach of Buddhism is to determine the nature of reality and distinguish truth from falsehood. Once the nature of reality has been understood in all its details, the means to progress on the spiritual path can be explained on that basis. Although the understanding of the nature of reality is not directly connected to the practice of the Way, in the end the purpose of its search turns out to be the practice itself. Scientific explanations can be of great assistance in helping us to establish the nature of reality and can ultimately be very useful in spiritual practice.

When you meet Western physicians and medical researchers, do you get the impression that the scientific method they use in experiments, which we call the scientific method, reflects their cultural origins, which are basically Christian or Judeo-Christian, and that as such their method explores only one aspect of biological and bacteriological reality? Or, on the contrary, do you have the impression that the slate has been wiped clean of Western religious and philosophical traditions, and that scientific method is therefore universal?

I think that scientists certainly have as their guiding principle to examine reality as objectively as possible, but despite this they are influenced by their own culture. The practitioner of science remains an individual, and consequently is influenced by his or her sociocultural environment; hence the importance of objective analysis. Does this answer your question?

Buddhism is sometimes presented in the West as a "rational religion," and this explanation seems capable of putting an end to the old debate often instigated by the religions of the Book—Judaism, Christianity, and Islam— with regard to the opposition between reason and faith. Do you think that a formula such as "rational religion" might signal a reconciliation of diverse spiritual traditions, and a better understanding of certain affinities between contemporary science and Buddhism, a spiritual path that, rightly or wrongly, seems as pragmatic as possible to us here in the West?

There are, according to Buddhist texts, in particular the *Abhidharma-kosha* by Vasubhandu, three different types of faith: "conviction faith," or confidence, "clear faith," or admiration, and "emulation faith." We can also speak of two sorts of faith. The first is founded on reason, which, when we examine the authentic foundations of that faith, will be found among those whose intelligence is sharpest. The other, more spontaneous and simple, is born of certain conventions among those of lesser intellectual faculties. Of the two, the former, founded on reason, is the more important. We can see, therefore, that reason and faith are intimately connected in Buddhism, since faith itself is generated on the basis of reason or logical comprehension.

There are several ways in which we can proceed with a logical analysis, depending on which of the three types of objects we are analyzing. In the first case, the object of analysis will be an apparent phenomenon. In the second, it will be hidden, and in the third, very hidden. These three types of objects correspond to the three types of existent phenomena. The manifest phenomena will be apprehended by initial perceptions known to be direct; the hidden phenomena by perceptions of the inferred type, based on irrefutable proof; and the very hidden phenomena by inferences founded on the validity accorded to the texts.

The significance of a very hidden phenomenon cannot be immediately determined by logical reasoning, and still less by sensory perception. We can only understand its meaning by relying upon what has been said by a dependable, trustworthy, and infallible third party, whose statements, to be believable, must be logical and must not contradict each other. Reason, which does not intervene directly to establish the existence of a phenomenon of the third type, does nevertheless have a role to play, insofar as we make use of it to determine the reliability of the person revealing the very hidden phenomenon.

This all goes to show that reason is always implicated in well-founded faith. I often have the opportunity to talk about this topic. With regard to religions essentially founded on "blind" faith, Buddhism is not a religion, but rather a science of mind, a form of atheism. Yet compared to radical materialism, it is indisputably a spiritual path.

It depends on our point of view. In summary, we might say that Buddhism is distinct from either of these approaches, or even that it is a bridge between them.

Over the last few years the physics community has shown increasing interest in questions dealing with the understanding of a reality which seems to escape scientists, despite the great precision and powers of prediction of modern theories, such as quantum physics. Generally a physicist seeks not only to report on appearances and the sequence of an event's cause and effect, but also to perfect an intelligible way of interpreting what we call "nature." Our creativity seems to depend largely on this. In order to accomplish this we create representations in terms of atoms, particles, forces, energies, space, time, etc.

The Buddhist tradition contains a great number of texts dealing with the nature of phenomena, discussing the reality of atoms, the nature of space and time. Would you explain to us why Buddhist teachings insist on this question? Do you feel it is important for scientists in their research to take into consideration the explication found in the Middle Way which refutes the inherent existence of phenomena?

This is why when followers of this school speak of negations they refute exclusive negations and admit only evocative negations. The followers of the Sautrantika school hold that certain phenomena, such as negations, are merely imputations or designations of discursive perceptions. This is the case, for example, with space, with compound phenomena dissociated from the form and the mind or the individual. Having said that, the meaning assigned here to the word "designation" or "imputation" differs slightly from that of the Madhyamika school, according to which all phenomena exist merely by simple imputation or designation.

According to the Chittamatra school, it does not matter whether we are speaking of the nominal basis of designation, of the nominal designation "form" applied to a form, or finally of the conceptual basis of the representative perception of the form as form—the form is believed not to exist by itself, in an exterior manner. However, if we look again at the earlier Sautrantika tradition, the form, as the conceptual basis of the representative perception apprehending it, exists by virtue of its own characteristics.

Up to this point, all Buddhist schools affirmed that all phenomena have an absolute existence. The followers of the Madhyamika school, however, refute the absolute existence of phenomena. Among these followers, those of the first sub-school, the Svatantrika, consider phenomena to exist conventionally, on their own. The other sub-school, the Prasangika, holds that even conventional phenomena do not exist through their own characteristics. All schools accept non-self, but the way in which it is conceived becomes progressively more and more subtle.

One question must be asked. If by "reality" we mean that once we have sought a designated object it can be found and is sufficient unto itself, then Buddhist philosophy denies the existence of such a reality. Reality does exist, however, if we define it as a situation where, although we cannot find the conceived object as such when we seek it, we nevertheless accept its existence as a designation. The Madhyamika or Middle Way philosophy places great emphasis upon the elimination of the two extremes.

What in physics is called "undiscovered" refers to a field which is infinitely partial and restricted in relation to the Buddhist notion of the "unfindable" character of the analyzed object. For Buddhists it is not enough to assert that the apprehension of self is false and that it will automatically disappear once we have understood that the object of our erroneous perception does not exist. We must eliminate this erroneous perception of our ego, that is, our apprehension of self, and not the perception of self as a simple designation. Why go to such trouble?

As I already explained briefly at an earlier stage, from this false perception an exaggerated vision of the ego will arise, one which is far removed from reality, and from that point we can divide the world in two: on the one hand, everything which has to do with self; and, on the other, everything else. We feel attachment for the first and aversion toward the second. It is precisely to weaken this attachment and aversion that we strive to eliminate the erroneous perception of the ego.

The Middle Way seeks principally to eliminate the two extremes of eternalism and nihilism. If we do not eliminate the extreme of eternalism we will not have the means to eliminate the false perception of our ego. At the other extreme, nihilism totally denies the existence of an ego. If we do not eliminate that extreme by reaching certainty with regard to the positive and negative aspects of an act and its agent on a conventional level, we will likewise reject the law of cause and effect, and that is something which is inadmissible. By ruling out the extreme of nihilism, we affirm that whoever creates or accumulates a cause must necessarily experience the results thereof. By refuting the extreme of eternalism, we avoid an exaggerated apprehension of the ego. This is the explanation of the Middle Way of the Madhyamika.

In short, we must endeavor to eliminate the erroneous perception of the ego and reinforce the correct view of the ego, without limiting ourselves to a strictly intellectual comprehension of these notions. Once we have understood this, we must continue to reflect and meditate on the subject so that a true inner transformation can take place. These notions will be more and more beneficial to us as our mind gradually becomes familiar with them.

You just said, a few minutes ago, that emotions can be a source of suffering. Do you have a definition for illness specific to Buddhism? Is illness the sign of an anomaly in one's biological or psychological behavior, or is it a physical disorder pointing to a psychological disorder? Isn't it normal that at certain times in life a human being will become ill? And what should the attitude of the medical profession be in these conditions; should it seek to remove the anomaly by any means possible, or help the human being live with it?

With regard to the states of mind sometimes referred to as "emotions," we can distinguish positive ones and negative ones. Thus, we say that feelings such as kindness, love, and compassion are positive emotions. But this is tantamount to saying that emotions subsist in the flow of consciousness of Buddhas, since such qualities emanate from their minds. This must not be confused with the affirmation that Buddhas are always concentrated on emptiness. Once Buddhahood is attained there is no longer any representative or discursive perception. What remains is direct comprehension of emptiness. But when they meditate on the wisdom of which emptiness is a part, all the qualities such as love and compassion are present in the minds of Buddhas.

As for the negative states of mind, we speak of the three main *kleshas*—afflicting emotions (literally, "poisons" of the mind)—attachment, aversion, and ignorance. From the point of view of a practicing Buddhist, these afflicting factors or mental poisons are the true mental illness. But we will not be cured of this illness until we achieve liberation. Before we reach that point, we will speak, therefore, of illness on a less subtle level.

In our society in general we consider a person to be perfectly healthy when his or her mind is not troubled or deeply perturbed by the three afflictions of the mind, even if these negative factors remain present in that person. It does occur, however, that under the influence of the three kleshas the mind, deeply disturbed, will lapse into confusion. At this point we can speak of mental illness. We distinguish two levels of mental illness: gross and subtle; both may be associated with physical illness. For this reason, Tibetan medicine regards a patient as a whole entity, taking into account not only his or her body but also his or her mind. This is why there are those who treat mental illness by combining Western psychotherapy with Buddhist methods. I think this is an excellent method.

Now, what should our response to illness be? It is perfectly obvious that all beings aspire to happiness and that they have every legitimate right to seek it. At the same time, they wish never to be afflicted by illness or any form of suffering whatsoever. We must try to prevent suffering and, in this context, preventive medicine is judicious. We must try to prevent illness in every way possible. If in spite of our efforts, certain conditions lead to illness and suffering, we must try to think clearly and not add to our suffering by worrying.

The film Why Did Bodhidharma Go to the East? *allowed us, through its very beautiful images, to gain experience and understanding of the extent to which spiritual liberation goes hand-in-hand with the enlightenment of consciousness that comes about in the interaction of human beings with their natural environment. But Buddhism also professes the absence of the actual existence of phenomena which, naively, we consider to be "natural." Would you tell us what place the idea of nature nonetheless occupies in Buddhism, and how the recognition of the emptiness of phenomena can lead us to alter our way of looking at the environment?*

It is said that inanimate objects do not have an inherent existence but a conventional one. This applies not only to inanimate objects but also to animate objects — that is, to beings endowed with consciousness. In this respect, the inanimate world is on an equal basis with the animate world of living beings. As far as the relation between the external world and the inner world (the mind) is concerned, according to certain philosophical schools, in particular the Yogacharya Svatantrika (a sub-school of Madhyamika) and the Chittamatra, external phenomena do not exist; all that exists is of the nature of the mind. Relativity is explained principally by the Prasangika branch of the Madhyamika school. According to the Madhyamika-Prasangika school, external phenomena exist and are not of the nature of the mind. They have no inherent or ultimate existence, but their nature is different from that of the mind. The outer world exists in dependence on the mind, insofar as it exists as a designation made by the mind. It does not, therefore, exist independently from the mind's imputation, nor is it of the nature of the mind. Therefore, an external world which can be examined objectively does exist.

Buddhism perceives the environment, in general, to be composed of infinitesimal particles; in particular, it views human beings as part of nature and for this reason there is, naturally, a link between humankind and our environment. Clearly, our happiness depends a great deal on the environment. This is why Buddhist texts explain how one should behave with regard to nature. For example, one of the monastic rules forbids the contamination or destruction of vegetation.

According to accounts of the Buddha's life, it would seem that he had a very deep relationship with nature. He was not born in the royal palace but in a park, under a sala tree. He attained complete enlightenment under the bodhi tree and left this earth to enter Parinirvana, again, between three sala trees. It would seem that the Buddha was very fond of trees.

Interest in the discoveries of modern astrophysics and the "big bang" theory reveal both a great fascination in the cosmos and a probing interrogation by members of our generation into their origins, their destiny, and the meaning of their existence. The "big bang" theory has had a significant impact on our way of looking at matter and nature; it has introduced considerable conceptual innovations. The formation of the structures of the universe, which function in interdependence, and which new research continues to reveal, is a seemingly endless source of wonder. Like all spiritual traditions, Buddhism conveys a cosmogonic myth. And yet Buddhism rejects the idea of creation. Why?

Most Western scientists think that life and consciousness are a magnificent result of the universe's material evolution, and yet they know neither how nor why matter emerged in such a way as to fulfill the conditions necessary to engender life and consciousness. What they do know is that these conditions are very strict, yet have nevertheless been fulfilled in our universe in an astonishing way. You have a very different point of view on this subject. Would you therefore speak to us about consciousness in its relation to matter and the universe?

Why is there no creation possible in Buddhism? It has been said that one cannot find living beings at the beginning of the universe for the essential reason that causes have no beginning. If there were a beginning to the universe, there would also have to be a beginning to consciousness. If we accepted a beginning to consciousness, we would also have to accept that its cause has a beginning, a sudden cause which would have instantly produced consciousness; this would lead to a great many other questions. If consciousness had arisen without cause, or from a permanent cause, that cause would have to exist on

a permanent basis, always, or not exist at all, ever. The fact that a phenomenon exists intermittently proves that it depends on causes and
conditions. When all the conditions are met, the phenomenon is produced. When those conditions are absent or incomplete, the phenomenon does not appear. As causes have no beginning and stretch
back to infinity, the same thing must apply for living beings. Creation is therefore not possible.

Let us now consider a particular phenomenon, a glacier for example: it does indeed have a beginning. How was it created? The outside world appears as a result of the acts of sentient beings who use
this world. These acts, or karmas, in turn originate in the intentions
and motivations of those beings who have not yet taken control of
their minds.

The "creator of the world," basically, is the mind. In the Sutras,
the mind is described as an agent. It is said that consciousness has no
beginning, but we must distinguish here between gross consciousness and subtle consciousness. Many gross consciousnesses appear as
dependents of the physical aggregates, of the body. This is evident
when you consider the different neurons and the functioning of the
brain, but just because physical conditions are met does not mean
that this is enough to produce a perception. In order for a perception
which will have the faculty to reflect and know an object to arise, it
must have a consubstantial cause. The fundamental consubstantial
cause, of the same substance as its result, will in this case be the subtle consciousness. It is this same consciousness or subtle mind which
penetrates the parental cells at the moment of conception. The subtle mind can have no beginning. If it had one, the mind would have
to be born of something that is not the mind. According to the
Kalachakra Tantra, one would have to return to the particles of space
to find the fundamental consubstantial causes of the external physical world as well as of the bodies of sentient beings.

Buddhist cosmology establishes the cycle of a universe in the following way: first there is a period of formation, then a period where
the universe endures, then another during which it is destroyed, followed by a period of void before the formation of a new universe.

During this void, the particles of space subsist, and from these particles the new universe will be formed. It is in these particles of space that we find the fundamental consubstantial cause of the entire physical world. If we wish to describe the formation of the universe and the physical bodies of beings, all we need do is analyze and comprehend the way in which the natural potential of different chemical and other elements constituting that universe was able to take shape from these space particles. It is on the basis of the specific potential of those particles that the structure of this universe and of the bodies of the beings present therein have come about. But from the moment the elements making up the world begin to set off different experiences of suffering and happiness among sentient beings, we must introduce the notion of karma—that is, positive and negative acts committed and accumulated in the past. It is difficult to determine where the natural expression of the potential of physical elements ends and the effect of karma—in other words, the result of our past acts—begins. If you wonder what the relation might be between karma and this external environment formed by natural laws, it is time to explain what karma is.

Karma means, first of all, action. We distinguish one type of karma which is of a mental nature, a mental factor of volition or intention. There also exist physical and oral karmas. To understand the connection between these physical, oral, or mental karmas and the material world, we must refer to the tantric texts. The Kalachakra Tantra in particular explains that in our bodies there are to be found, at gross, subtle, and extremely subtle levels, the five elements which make up the substance of the external world. It is therefore in this context, I believe, that we must envision the connection between our physical, oral, and mental karmas, and the external elements.

I have yet another doctor's question for you. In France, and in the medical field in particular, we often hear of The Tibetan Book of the Dead. *Many current medical techniques such as reanimation, surgery, transplants, and intensive chemotherapy in cancer treatment, contribute to the notion that a patient's death is a failure on the part of medicine. In France, for example, 70 percent of deaths occur in hospitals, where the last days of a patient's life are often spent in intensive care. For this reason, we do not often speak to the patient about his or her imminent death; on the contrary, everything is done so as to sustain the patient's hope and will to live. It would seem, moreover, that it is important to keep hope alive, but in a number of cultures, including, if I have understood it correctly, the Buddhist tradition, preparation for death is part of a human being's rights and responsibilities.*

In your opinion, is death a biological and medical event, or is it simply personal and spiritual? Is it right that we do everything in our power to save or at least prolong for a few years the life of a human being? Or conversely, is it unfair to impose the risk that death will occur in a highly technical medical context, where the patient is cut off from family and friends? According to a report of the World Health Organization, life is not absolutely good, nor is death absolutely bad. What is your position on this? And finally, do the efforts of Western medicine to thwart death seem questionable to you? If, on the contrary, death belongs to the dying and their close friends and family, at what point should the physician withdraw? Under what conditions must we inform the patient that death can no longer be avoided?

First of all, we should realize that death is truly part of life and that it is neither good nor bad in itself. *The Tibetan Book of the Dead,* to which you just referred, has this to say: "What we call death is merely a concept." In other words, death represents the end of the gross consciousness and its support, the gross body. This happens at the gross level of the mind. But neither death nor birth exist at the subtle level of consciousness that we call "clear light." Of course, generally speaking, death is something we dread. However, death, which we want nothing to do with, is unavoidable. This is why it is important that during our lifetime we become familiar with the idea of death, so that it will not be a real shock to us at the moment it comes. We do not meditate regularly on death in order to die more quickly; on the contrary, like everyone, we wish to live a long time. However, since death is inevitable, we believe that if we began to prepare for it at an earlier point in time, on the day of our death it will be easier to accept it.

I think that there is no general rule with regard to the intensive care often given to patients in order to prolong their lives. It is a complex problem, and in examining it we must take numerous elements into account, according to each set of circumstances, each particular case. For example, if we prolong the life of a person who is critically ill but whose mind remains very lucid, we are giving him or her the opportunity to continue to think in the way only a human being can think. We must also consider whether the person will benefit from prolonged life or whether, on the contrary, he will experience great physical and moral suffering, physical pain, or extreme fear. If the person is in a deep coma, that is yet another problem. The wishes of the patient's family must also be taken into account, as well as the immense financial problems that prolonged care can create. I think the most important thing is to try and do our best to ensure that the dying person may depart quietly, with serenity and inner peace. There is also a distinction to be made between those dying people who practice a religion and those who do not. Whatever the case, whether one is religious or not, I believe it is better to die in peace.

PHYSICAL PHENOMENA AND THE CONSCIOUSNESS OF PHENOMENA

We have the unique opportunity to examine, together with the Dalai Lama, some issues dealing with the heart of scientific practice from the point of view of interdependence. Before we begin this discussion, would His Holiness explain in a few words the meaning of interdependence in Buddhist philosophy and what you hope to take with you from this symposium?

I have learned a great many things from my encounters with scientists of all sorts and have profited greatly from these meetings. Certain Buddhist explanations have also proven useful to scientists, insofar as they have enabled them to consider their specializations from another perspective. Most of you, I believe, are familiar with the elementary

Buddhist approach, in particular that of the Mahayana, where we should initially be skeptical, then probe the question, and finally accept it once we are convinced of its veracity. We even have the right—with, of course, as we are Buddhists, the highest respect—to refute the teachings of the Buddha if our discoveries contradict them. As you can see, we are, in a way, free to have a critical mind, even with regard to our own philosophy. In such a context I see no obstacles to engaging in dialogues with scientists or even with radical materialists. On the contrary, this is a very good thing.

In addition, there are, in my experience, certain ideas which we take for granted. As a result, our reasoning process remains insufficient. Critical questions which make us think about the subjects concerned are therefore very useful. For people who are brought up in a Buddhist culture, certain concepts are self-evident. Because of this, we sometimes neglect to follow the entire thread of complex reasoning to its conclusion. This is why questions raised by people of diverse disciplines oblige us to envision these question in a new way.

To begin with, I would like to present briefly the Buddhist view of interdependence. We may comprehend this principle, also called dependent origination, on different levels, beginning with that of causality, the law of cause and effect accepted by all four schools of Buddhist philosophy. There is another way to understand this principle, to see it in relation to the fact that a whole depends on its parts. Indeed, any existent thing is considered to be a whole, that is, composed of parts. Since it is made up of parts, it depends upon them. Its very existence depends on its parts and it cannot exist in an autonomous or independent manner.

To give a better explanation of the principle of interdependence, we must place it in the context of the Buddhist description of reality. First of all, all existent phenomena are either permanent or impermanent. There is no third possibility. Among the impermanent phenomena we find physical phenomena, also called "form," and non-physical existents which include, on the one hand, mental phenomena (the mind), and on the other, abstract phenomena, known as "compound phenomena dissociated from form and mind." The interdependence of physical phenomena is defined in relation to space; such phenomena depend on their directional parts. The interdependence of non-physical phenomena is envisioned in relation to time or even according to spatial directions. The mind, for example, is a succession of moments. We speak of a mental continuum. We say of compound phenomena dissociated from form and mind that they also depend on their directional parts. As for non-compound space itself, we speak of the south of space, the east, etc.

I have been presenting the principle of interdependence in a general manner according to the Madhyamika school, the Middle Way, which includes two sub-schools, of which the Prasangika school (the "Consequentialists") is the higher. This school adds an even more subtle explanation to existing interpretations of dependent origination—that of the unfindableness, the "undetectability," of any designated existent thing whatever. In other words, when through analytical method we seek the phenomenon behind its appearance, it is unfindable. However, if it is said that existents are unfindable after they have been sought through analytical process, should we then conclude that they do not exist at all? To abandon this nihilistic view, we will answer with a categorical "No." Phenomena exist—not in an autonomous way, per se, but rather in a relation of dependency with other phenomena, such as the name by which they are designated. This is the most profound way to understand the principle of interdependence. Phenomena exist, therefore, as denominations. No phenomena exist otherwise. However, everything which can be designated by the mind does not necessarily exist. The most difficult thing is to determine, among all the things imputed by the mind, which ones exist and which do not. Even while we deny the autonomous and independent status of existents, we must not fall into the trap of an exaggerated relativism in which everything the mind conceives of is real. The problem now is to determine which criteria will enable us to find out which phenomena among all those designated by the mind actually do exist.

The Prasangika texts describe three such criteria: a phenomenon conceived by the mind is said to exist, first of all, if it is admitted by an immediate, non-discursive perception; then, if this immediate perception is not contradicted by a known perception which observes the conventional plan; and finally, if its existence is not negated by the analytical mind which examines the ultimate mode of existence of a phenomenon. According to these three criteria we can determine whether or not a phenomenon exists conventionally. These criteria refer solely to the mind perceiving the object in question, and this reminds us once again that nothing can exist independently from the mind which perceives it.

This obliges us to delimit the notion of known perception. For all the schools, with the exception of the Prasangika school, a known perception apprehends its object without the slightest error or inaccuracy. These schools tolerate no element of inaccuracy in a known perception, whereas the Prasangika school of the Middle Way affirms that, although a known perception cannot err in the acknowledgment of the apprehended object, an element of inaccuracy may nevertheless be present. Let us take, for example, the case of the known discursive perception of the impermanence of sound: this experience, which occurs solely in relation to the object apprehended—the impermanence of the phenomenon of sound—is nonetheless inexact for followers of the Prasangika school, because they hold its object to be endowed, moreover, with an absolute, independent existence. All the other schools accept the inherent existence of conventional reality. So for them the perception that phenomena exist in this way is correct, just as the known perception is from all aspects correct and exact. According to the Prasangika school, the only perfectly accurate perception, free of any form of error, is the direct and convincing experience of emptiness—that is, the non-representative perception of the ultimate nature of phenomena.

This has been a brief presentation of the principle of interdependence.

I would like to tell you a parable that compares classical and quantum physics. Say there is a fisherman fishing in a very muddy pond. From the classical point of view, there is an invisible fish swimming around; it is only invisible because the pond is muddy. Of course the man can catch it, and then he will see it hanging from his line. In this view, the fish was perfectly localized and had only a local interaction with the water of the pond. However, from the quantum point of view, the fish dissolves in the pond and ceases to be perfectly localized. It has a kind of interaction with the entire pond, all the time. In some cases it can have a very strong interaction with a very great volume, the entire ocean for example. If the fisherman manages to catch the fish, a phenomenon of localization occurs, and he will see an ordinary fish hanging from his line. But when he places the fish upon the grass, the fish dissolves again as soon as the fisherman ceases to look at it.

Do you believe that this quantum point of view, where every microscopic particle possesses a kind of knowledge of the entire space surrounding it, as described by the underlying mathematics, is richer than the classical point of view? Do you believe it can clarify the concept of the parts of a composite body in a more subtle manner than the classical approach? I am very interested in any comments you might have on the quantum point of view with regard to interdependence.

I can sense, at a very deep level, a certain number of convergences between the quantum view of reality and the Buddhist understanding of interdependence, but I do not yet have a very clear understanding of this quantum view. Although I have tried my hardest to understand it, I still encounter certain problems! Therefore I do not feel sure enough of myself in this domain to establish a parallel. However, from your description it seems to me that there are resemblances between the quantum view of reality and a concept specific to one of the schools of Buddhist philosophy, the Chittamatra, or "Mind Only," school.

According to this school, the outside world, the physical universe, is not produced externally but is of the nature of the mind alone. To defend this thesis, they use the argument of the simultaneity of the object and the perception which apprehends it. In other words, every time you observe something, the observation of the object and the object itself are simultaneous. Thus, the object exists only when it is perceived. The Prasangika school, however, does not accept this view, according to which the external world would ultimately be nothing more than a simple projection of the mind, for this leads to numerous philosophical and logical inconsistencies.

We might perhaps establish an interesting parallel between quantum mechanics, in which reality is described as fluid rather than solid, and a particular type of meditation on matter, where the meditator concentrates his attention on the nature of an object at a microscopic level as being a form composed of infinitesimal particles. After prolonged practice, the perception of the particles that make up the object becomes so sharp that the meditator no longer feels its solidity, even if he touches it, whereas another person will continue to feel the solidity of that same object. People meditating have actually had this experience of the physical world; this is not just a theoretical description.

Referring still to meditative experience, it is possible for individuals to travel through space. Space is conventionally defined in terms of voidness and the absence of contact and obstruction. Although it is not formed of gross physical elements, if a meditator concentrates on the infinitesimal particles which make up space—the directional parts, for example, and the subtle solidity of these particles— because they cannot overlap, the meditator will, after intensive training, eventually be able to walk upon them. Here, too, we are talking about the experiential point of view of the meditator. Since these unusual occurrences are in the realm of possibility for a meditator, it would be interesting to know whether quantum mechanics could explain these phenomena.

In practice, the physicist is neither a robot nor a computer. Even if we can maneuver a piston with a robot and calculate everything the machine is doing with a computer, the physicist is still a human being. Someone trying to find the correct way to deal with a problem is not in a situation of absolute objectivity and rationality—those remain to be discovered. We will always have desires, including the desire for truth, which will interfere with our attempts to discover rationality and our way of dealing with a situation, if in fact we could carry out our experiment like a robot.

My question has to do with this: it seems to me that the practice of physics apparently requires a sort of asceticism. This is how I define asceticism: it aims to control desires in order to better serve the truth. First of all, can we use this word, "asceticism," which is perhaps a very Western word, to describe this? Please comment on these notions of interdependence and the way in which we treat it.

In fact, the problem you describe in your experiments and your research into the nature of reality is a problem we all confront in our daily lives. If we had to wait to know in detail all the elements which make up reality before we act, we would never act! We must therefore find a compromise.

I have the feeling that it would be difficult to reach the stage where we could give a complete and definitive description of reality. Although I do not fully grasp the description of reality given by quantum mechanics, it seems to me, as far as I can tell, that at the heart of this reality one finds that nature at the most subtle level is unpredictable. When we look for rules of behavior they do not make sense. There are changes that are impossible to explain, which seem to occur by chance or for reasons we are still ignorant of. For this reason, as a Buddhist I wonder if the intervening factor that might explain these abrupt changes might not be the karmic principle, the law of causality. More precisely, it seems to me that such unpredictability might be explained by the existence of even more subtle elements influencing this behavior than by those we have already observed, as well as by karma which would play a role. Having said that, the effect of karma can be neither measured nor quantified.

To what kind of reality, if there is such, do you feel most drawn?

The Buddhist answer to the question, "What exactly is reality?" is simple and direct: it is of an interdependent nature! When we use the term "reality" in a Buddhist context, we must specify which level of reality we are referring to. If we remain on the specific level of the world of phenomena, what we call relative or conventional truth, we can then describe this reality in very complex terms and in a very detailed way. But on a general level, to describe the general traits of reality and its ultimate nature, we would see on the one hand that it is not produced by its own characteristics and that it is devoid of inherent or absolute existence, and on the other hand that it is of an interdependent nature. In Buddhist terms, both emptiness (or the absence of inherent existence) and interdependence are like the two sides of a coin.

When we speak of reality on the specific level of conventional truth, we are entering a realm of great complexity. For example, if we ask Buddhist philosophers to define a particular object, they will provide a coherent, convincing definition of that object, enumerating its attributes in a more or less complete manner. They will give the principal characteristics of the object in question and add "among others." If we point out to them that the list is not complete, they reply that such a list would include all existing phenomena because the object exists in relation to all of them.

With this subject it is fairly important to understand the relation of language and concepts to phenomena. It is a question of overall complexity. According to Buddhist logic, language and concepts understand reality through a process of elimination of what the object is not. Language and concepts define an object by a process of elimination of other phenomena, not by simple affirmation. Representative perception—perception through mental image—of a vase, for example, occurs through the mental elimination of what the vase is not. And for a definition to be complete it would therefore be necessary to name all the phenomena which are not the existent in question, which is impossible.

The following quotes show how difficult it is to distinguish between quantum mechanics and Buddhist understanding. First, from a Pali text:

> Vasha asked the Buddha: "Do you maintain that the soul of a saint exists after death?"
>
> "I do not maintain that the soul of a saint exists after death."
>
> "Do you maintain that the soul of a saint does not exist after death?"

"I do not maintain that the soul of a saint does not exist after death."
"Where is the saint reborn?"
"It is not appropriate to say that the saint has been reborn."
"Therefore he has not been reborn?"
"It is not appropriate to say that the saint has not been reborn."

Now, an excerpt from Oppenheimer's book Science and Understanding:

When we ask, for example, if the position of the electron remains the same, we must say no. When we ask if the position of the electron changes over time, we must say no. When we ask if the position of the electron is at rest, we must say no. When we ask if it is moving, we must say no.

Finally, this saying by Maiyetri, a philosopher queen of ancient India, from 3,000 years ago, which concerns her search for reality. She says:

Guide me from the unreal to the real.
Guide me from obscurity to light.
Guide me from death to immortality.

Don't scientific truths reveal a structure of the universe, with its hidden truths to be unearthed like ancestral treasures? Or are we scientists, physicists in particular, like magicians pulling rabbits out of the hats we have hidden them in? A good Buddhist might say that both hat and rabbit are unreal. I might add that magic is real. What do you think?

Among the qualities of a Buddha described in Buddhist texts we find omniscience. Well, there can only be omniscience if there is something to know. It is also written in these texts that knowable things have two aspects: their ultimate nature and their relative, or conventional, truth. We also find affirmations by the Indian masters such as this by Nagarjuna: "It is only through understanding the two truths that one can attain liberation. If we ignore them we cannot attain liberation." The difference between liberation (Sanskrit: *moksha*), the state of being liberated, and its opposite, samsara, the state of ignorance and servitude, is our knowledge or ignorance of the ultimate nature of phenomena—emptiness.

To describe the omniscience of a Buddha, we will speak of the twenty-one categories of profound and penetrating wisdom, elaborated in 146 types of superior wisdom. This is all based on the supposition that there is something to know, for otherwise we could not speak of knowledge or wisdom.

The passage quoted above is taken from a sutra where fourteen questions without answers are enumerated. In his text called *Prajnamula*, "The Foundations of Wisdom," the Indian philosopher Nagarjuna commented at length on this subject and proposed certain criteria according to which it is possible to understand why the Buddha did not reply to certain questions. Among other things, Nagarjuna explained that when an affirmative or negative reply to a question would necessarily lead the person with whom he was speaking to views either of eternalism or nihilism, the Buddha preferred to remain silent.

In the same vein, we can find in Buddhist logic a four-fold reasoning applied to the notion of emptiness which allows us to reach the conclusion that it is devoid of the four false views. These four extreme views are absolute existence, total nonexistence, both absolute existence and total nonexistence, and neither absolute existence nor total nonexistence. If phenomena did not exist on a conventional level, such reasoning, particularly where the extreme view of complete nonexistence is concerned, would serve no purpose. My answer to the question is that there exists a reality of phenomena which we can understand and approach.

With regard to existence and nonexistence, Nagarjuna states clearly in one of his texts that to deny the absence of inherent existence is the same as affirming inherent existence. This is a logical principle applied to phenomena of a directly contradictory nature, where not only does the negation of one thing affirm its opposite, but also where a third possibility cannot be envisioned. Kamalashila, a disciple of the great philosopher Shantirakshita, defends the same point of view in "The Middle Ornament." The position of the Madhyamika-Prasangika on this question of the nature of reality is very complex.

It refutes any inherent, autonomous status ordinarily granted to existent phenomena. Phenomena exist, but in interdependence, as denominations. Do not conclude from this that everything the mind imagines exists. Not only does not everything conceived by the mind necessarily exist, but karma also has a limited application. In actual fact, the law of causality does not intervene at a certain level of reality. Buddhist philosophy envisions four fundamental principles, including that of the specific nature of an existent. Take, for example, continuity: the fact that previous moments lead to subsequent moments is a natural process which has nothing to do with karma.

So we realize how, according to the Madhyamika-Prasangika, we must "walk on a thread" and find a happy medium between the extreme view of nihilism, in which phenomena have no existence, and the extreme view of eternalism, in which phenomena have an existence purported to be independent and absolute.

The question of interdependence doesn't concern only the status of objects in each world—for example, of objects in physics—but also and above all the status of each of these worlds insofar as they are a pragmatic result of symbolic constructions, interlocutory strategies, and interactional practices. I have no answer to this question so I would like to ask His Holiness for one. Are there points of convergence between the nondualistic logic of Buddhist thought, its insistence on emptiness or the absence of foundations, and contemporary thought, which I have characterized as a relational apprehension of objects, a relativist conception of truths, and the acceptance of a plurality of forms of rationality as well as of a multiplicity of worlds?

In the context of the question you have raised, I would like once again to insist upon the necessity, from a Buddhist point of view, of preserving a happy medium between the extremes of nihilism and eternalism, a middle view which affirms the existence of phenomena as denominations and rejects their absolute existence. This philosophical point is perceived as the most difficult to realize, according to the Prasangika view. In other words, the difficulty does not reside so much in the negation of the inherent existence of phenomena as in the comprehension of what remains behind—the residue.

When the notion of duality is evoked in a Buddhist context, the various connotations covered by this term must be taken into account. For example, we can speak of a nondual perception which simultaneously perceives both truths, relative and ultimate; we can speak of a nondual perception meaning the direct perception of an object without the intermediary of a mental image; and finally, we can speak of a nondual perception signifying that its object of perception no longer appears as an independent and autonomous entity. The ultimate level of nonduality is superior wisdom—non-conceptual, free of any duality whatsoever. This wisdom, displayed as part of a meditative experience, has no relation to an ordinary perception of conventional reality.

I would like to comment on what I have heard in the participants' arguments up to now. I have the feeling, and I may be wrong, that Western thought has a tendency to move from one extreme to the other. It is as if according to the classical models of science and technology, a pressing need was felt in the past to find solid foundations and absolute truths, whereas this type of research is, nowadays, most often considered be futile. There has been a complete reversal, heading off toward another extreme—relativism, where nothing, ultimately, exists any longer, where perhaps there is no longer even any reality as such! It seems that the possibility that gray areas may exist between the two extremes has not been taken into consideration. This is what I have observed. There is often talk of the disparity between our perception of the world and reality; the very idea of contradiction between the manner in which we see the world and that in which phenomena exist allows us to infer the existence of a certain degree of reality.

Next!

Given the fact that in your tradition there exist states of clarity, and there are reports of people experiencing this more subtle state of mind, my question is two-fold: first, do you think that such non-cognitive states of mind could in theory be observed with our external tools? For example, if we were to place a meditator who is in a state of clear light into one of our modern machines with magnetic resonance, using new brain-imaging techniques, would we be able to see something, some sign of this subtle state? Perhaps we do not yet know how to do this but, in theory, do you think it would it be possible?

If so, what, in your opinion, would be the relation between the two levels, gross and subtle, in the field of interdependence? We do not want to succumb to a new dualism, that of grossness and subtlety. What is the nature of causality between these two levels?

I think it may be difficult to measure the activity specific to the mind that consists of reflecting one's object and knowing it. But as the experiences of the gross consciousness appear in the activity of the brain and can therefore be observed as such, it seems to me that it should also be possible to study the physical manifestations of the more subtle states of mind. The subtle level of consciousness, referred to by the term "clear light," appears among other things at the moment of death. Those who have practiced ahead of time are able to remain voluntarily in this state for several days after death, and for the duration of this time their bodies do not decompose. Modern scientific instruments would be able to observe this phenomenon, and in fact this has already occurred in India. Although it seems to me that it would be difficult to observe the subtle mind in its entirety using these methods, I think all the same that this might give us an idea.

To answer the second question, concerning the relation between the gross mind and the subtle mind, you must know that the degree of subtlety of the mind will depend in part on the degree of subtlety of its physical support and on the particular ruling condition, the six senses. But the faculty shared by all perceptions—to reflect an object and know it—comes from the subtle mind. In this way it is possible to understand the fundamental relation that exists between the subtle and gross levels of the mind. Sensory and mental consciousnesses are produced depending on ruling conditions specific to each of the six senses: visual sense for visual perceptions, mental faculty or sense for mental knowledge, etc. Because the grossness of their support is greater, sensory perceptions are relatively gross compared to mental consciousnesses. Still, all have the ability to reflect their object and know it, an aptitude which derives from their common underlying foundation, the subtle mind, clear light. The tantric texts of Buddhism comment on the manner in which the gross levels of the mind are linked to the subtle mind. It is explained how eighty states of consciousness correspond to four stages of absorption of the gross mind into the subtle mind, during death for example. The links between the different levels of the mind are illustrated, but it is a very complex subject which would be difficult to go into at this point.

I am particularly interested in the question of the validation of phenomena by consciousness, and therefore in the conditions of their integration. I would like to ask if, apart from certain limited analogies—which are very interesting—between the Dharma and contemporary sciences, Buddhism has something more fundamental to offer the West. I am thinking here of the practice of meditation in particular: a renewed open-mindedness and sense of space and time which might give scientific information access to a more truly conscious "reality," so that it would no longer be merely a fascinating "fiction" related to matter/energy, the space/time curve, the nonsubstantiality of phenomena, etc.

I have no immediate answer to your question, but I do have a few ideas to put before you. It would be interesting to refer some of these ideas to certain types of phenomena mentioned by Buddhist philosophical texts. There are physical phenomena, forms, which are not made up of gross matter (one of the properties of which is solid obstruction), but which are, rather, subtle forms, which may be classified into five categories. The first are forms deriving from an assembly, infinitesimal particles such as atoms. Their form is described as being spherical, but their color is not mentioned. Next we have the mental appearances of space, that is the appearance with which the sky appears to mental perception. I think that modern science could provide more explanations on this subject and have greater success in making it comprehensible. Will it, in reality be particles of space or of light? These two first types of subtle physical phenomena are accepted by all and are not solely creations of the mind.

The third type of subtle form includes those which are imagined and might appear, for example, to a person meditating, but which only the meditator can see and which cannot fulfill their usual functions. The next category is that of forms created by the powers of concentration; these are phenomena which originate from the four physical elements through the force of meditation practiced by those who have been very successful in developing their powers of concentration. These phenomena may be experienced not only by the meditator but also by other people. Through meditating in this way it is possible to create fire, for example — fire which can fulfill its function of burning and heating. It may seem strange, to say the least, that forms can be produced through the power of concentration. I do not know exactly how they can be interpreted or understood, but I do not think they last for very long after they have been created, probably only for the duration of the meditation. These third and fourth types of form should give scientists matter for reflection! If these phenomena exist, how are they produced?

Up to now we have talked about information contained in the Sutras. We could also examine them in the light of the Tantras, the esoteric aspect of Buddhism which deals at length with the nature of more or less subtle energies.

REALITY AND ILLUSION

What is the concept of time in Buddhism?

Excuse me, I misunderstood the Tibetan translation of the question; in our language the words for "demon" and "time" are pronounced almost identically, and I was about to give you a talk about what a demon is from a Buddhist point of view!

Regarding the Buddhist concept of time, our philosophy has

adopted several positions. The Sautantrika school, also known as the "Holders of Discourse," affirms that all phenomena and events exist only in the present moment. For this school, past and future are nothing other than simple concepts, simple mental constructs. As for the Madhyamika-Prasangika school, the Consequence School of the Middle Way, it generally explains time in terms of relativity, as an abstract entity developed by the mind on the basis of an imputation, the continuity of an event or phenomenon. This philosophical view describes, therefore, an abstract concept whose function is dependent on the continuum of phenomena. From this point on, to try to explain time as an autonomous entity, independent from an existing object, proves impossible. That time is a relative phenomenon and can claim no independent status is quite clear; I often give the example of external objects which can be easily conceived of in terms of the past or future, but of which the very present seems inconceivable. We can divide time into centuries, decades, years, days, hours, minutes, and seconds. But as the second is also divisible into multiple parts, milliseconds for example, we can easily lose our grasp of the notion of present time!

As for consciousness, it has neither past nor future and knows only present moments; it is the continuum of a present moment being transformed into another present moment, whereas with external objects the present disappears in favor of notions of past and future. But further pursuit of this logic will lead to absurdity, because to situate past and future we need a frame of reference which, in this case, is the present, and we have just lost its trace in fractions of milliseconds. . . .

If consciousness has neither beginning nor end, and if it is not permanent, does it age like an old house, changing with each moment? And if it has neither form, nor color, nor odor, how can it be transformed?

First of all, let us try to agree on the problematic notion of consciousness, of the mind. We have only a gross and partial intellectual understanding of consciousness. Our desire to perfect that understanding through analytical research will lead us to the discovery of the luminous, clear, and knowing nature of consciousness. It is extremely important to know how to identify clearly the object we are analyzing, in this case the nature of consciousness. Once we identify the nature of consciousness with its immaterial and nonobstructive characteristics, we will be able to use it to confront external objects and a third category of phenomena, abstract concepts such as the notions of time and change which have neither the nature of consciousness nor that of material objects. Keeping these three classifications well in mind—physical objects, the mind, and abstract mental constructs—we will be able to identify consciousness by comparing it to the two other categories of phenomena. Once we have clear knowledge of its nature, it will not only be possible to have a conscious experience of the process of change occurring within consciousness, but also to understand how consciousness and the experience of consciousness depend on a preceding moment of consciousness. Only the preceding instant of consciousness may lead to a subsequent moment of consciousness—nothing else has that faculty.

I do not think we can talk about the continuity of consciousness solely in terms of chronology. The very idea of chronology, and thus aging, only has meaning in relation to material phenomena, such as the body. On the level of different individual consciousnesses, such as sensory faculties, we can use the term "aging" to refer to the physiological basis, the body of a human being; in the case of sensory consciousnesses, aging in large part progresses in keeping with the individual's physiological condition. The two evolutions are not independent. To speak of the "aging of sensory consciousnesses" is possible if we associate this affirmation with a biological, physiological process, something we cannot do when we speak of mental consciousness.

I think it is very important to reflect on the nature of consciousness, to know the different types of consciousnesses and their natures. Buddhist scripture holds that sensory perceptions, such as visual consciousness, are direct and not conceptual; a visual perception perceives a form, without however discerning between its good or bad, desirable or undesirable, aspects. The discernment takes place on a conceptual level, which constitutes a far more interpretative process than that of simple sensory perception.

As far as mental consciousness, the world of conceptual thought, is concerned, we distinguish different levels of subtlety, from the gross to the most subtle, well-documented in the tantric system. The brain, neurons, synapses, etc., are connected to consciousness, and this opens onto a vast terrain for investigation when we connect them with what tantric literature calls energy (Tibetan: *lung;* Sanskrit: *prana*).

Research into the exact nature of the relation between the brain, consciousness, and energy proves to be very interesting. When all the functions of the brain have stopped and physiological conditions have disappeared, it would seem that a form of the process of consciousness continues to exist. This has been observed in the experience of certain realized lamas whose bodies, although declared clinically dead, do not decompose and remain fresh for several days or even several weeks. At this stage, the Buddhist point of view maintains that the individual is not altogether dead, that he is continuing to evolve through the process of death, and that he remains in a state of subtle consciousness. I think scientists ought to seek logical explanations for these cases when the body does not decompose even when the functions of the brain and the body have stopped.

The texts also give accounts of meditators who have learned to develop a supernatural ability to create physical objects with their mind, or produce elements such as fire and air, perceived not only by their creator but also, apparently, by other people. Other types of mentally created objects are only perceived by the meditator. I do wonder what the substantial, material cause of these external objects might be. If there is a result—a mentally created physical object—it must be preceded by a cause and conditions of the same nature. I also wonder if these objects exist solely during the practitioner's meditation, and cease to exist as soon as he leaves his meditative absorption. I cannot say what the material cause of this type of mentally created object might be. It is a question I address to the monastic community: can consciousness become a substantial cause of material objects? The Tantras, such as that of Guyasamaja, speak of the illusory body and its substantial cause, which is purported to be subtle energy, as subtle energy is part of the material world. I must say that this problem leaves me puzzled.

How did illusion begin?

As the continuum of the mind has no beginning, ignorance does not have one either. If it did, we would have to discover from within a state of consciousness that predates ignorance and is different from it—in an enlightened mind, therefore—a cause resulting in ignorance. This makes no sense.

Is there a primordial cause for all causes?

No. Generally, causes have no origin, and for this reason effects have none either. We can nevertheless say, in the context of a very specific point, that in some cases causes and effects have a beginning. When we establish that the continuum of the mind is without beginning, to want to discern a beginning to causes would be an obvious contradiction! You know, Buddhist logicians are quite rigorous. From the moment they accept that the mind has no beginning they can affirm logically and resolutely that neither causes nor effects have one either.

The perception of the world that human beings have is very different from that of creatures such as insects, for example. Is there a world which exists independently from these differing perceptions? What does a Buddha perceive? Does the world depend on the different forms of consciousnesses that perceive it, or does it exist only through sensory experiences?

This is a complex question. Let us try to answer it from the point of view of human perception by using the example of an object. A human being will have a certain perception, which will in fact only be partial, since he cannot see the object from every angle; animals also have these limitations. Yet we can certify that we perceive the object. The important thing to remember is that our perception of the world is influenced by a false apprehension, that of the true existence of phenomena.

As for a Buddha's perception, it is very difficult to say what it might be. One thing is certain: a Buddha's perception of the world is free from any of the projections we ordinarily make—free of the apprehension of the world, of phenomena and of events, because it exists independently and autonomously from the mind which perceives it. To think of an object of perception as independent from the mind which perceives it leads us to question whether or not we should accept a reality external to the mind. This subject has been treated at length in Buddhist philosophy. It does not seem that the existence of a particular object need necessarily be accompanied by its perception. Let us imagine, for example, that there is no one in this room and that this text is lying on the table. It will remain here even if there is no one to look at it.

We can of course discuss many phenomena which may seem difficult to fathom, and of which we do not have a clear understanding. But it is hardly coherent to assert that a phenomenon can exist in a totally autonomous manner, independently from perceptions and from the mind. Such a position seems, in my opinion, difficult to defend. From a Buddhist point of view, no phenomena exist which cannot be perceived by the mind of a Buddha. Leaving aside the omniscient mind of an Enlightened One, a domain which we can neither imagine nor conceive of, let us take the case of a thing or a phenomenon which to one person might be totally incomprehensible, to another vaguely clear, and to a third, quite apparent. This example is a good illustration of the idea that an external world completely independent from perceptions or the mind is impossible.

I am going to tell you the story of two students who lived in Tibet. One said to the other that he had a question of a philosophical nature to ask: "Is the pillar of this temple a mental construct? If no one remains in this room, does the pillar continue to be a conceptual imputation? I have my doubts on this subject." The other student replied that he had raised a fairly difficult point, but that one could think that if the pillar was a mental construct, the consciousness designating it would have no need to remain attached to it because in fact it is always with the pillar. By analogy, those who study such texts are called students. But they need not remain seated by the texts in order to continue to go by that name; whether they are sleeping, eating, or going for walks, the label "student" can still be applied.

If we see reality, do we not also see duality? In other words, how can a mind in which there is no longer any duality perceive the existence of duality, for example, among those who suffer?

Duality can be understood at different levels: duality of subject and object, duality of distinct separation, duality of conventional appearances—that is, of the relative world. The mind of a Buddha is free of all conceptual imagery and thus from any dualist projection. Although it is also free from the duality separating the subject from the object, a Buddha's perception of the conventional world has not disappeared altogether. As long as he is situated on the level of dualism dissociating the phenomenal world of appearances from its underlying emptiness, he will have the perception and the experience of the relative world. But this mode of enlightened perception is completely different from that of ordinary beings—from our own. We perceive phenomena and events as if they had an independent existence, as if they were in possession of a true autonomous and inherent nature. Although a Buddha is free from this fundamental ignorance, his omniscient mind understands, of course, the mind of an ordinary being, veiled by illusion, and which takes the appearance of phenomena, along with the appearances they perceive, as reality.

The conventional world can be divided into two categories— defiled phenomena and undefiled phenomena—which can be interpreted in various ways. We may, however, affirm that any form of experience defiled by the instinctive habits of ignorance and by an apprehension of reality as an inherent and independent entity is considered to be defiled or polluted. It is in this way that most phenomena of the conventional world are perceived. The distinctive traits of a Buddha, on the other hand, such as his eighty major and minor marks, are undefiled phenomena because they are the pure characteristics of an enlightened and omniscient mind. They are said to be pure because even at the level of their cause there are no defilements to be found. When the physical manifestation of a Buddha appears to human beings, there are on his part no traces of those impurities which we find in the ordinary mode of perception of human beings who, influenced by the ignorant apprehension of the inherent and autonomous existence of things and events, will continue to project this false apprehension onto the very qualities of a Buddha.

As to whether or not the perceptions of ordinary beings, simple products of their veiled minds, can appear to Buddhas, I would reply in the negative: an Enlightened One knows that beings have a mind affected by false perceptions, but he himself does not have these misguided perceptions. To the question, "Can a Buddha experience suffering?", we can only reply once again in the negative, because Buddhahood is liberation from suffering, the cessation of all suffering; but this does not mean that a Buddha is incapable of perceiving suffering. He has realized great compassion and is in a position of empathy with the suffering of sentient beings. To conclude, we must know how to make the distinction between the perception of a Buddha's perception and our personal experience.

How can different Buddhas exist if they have eliminated all the causes and conditions leading to samsara or nirvana? Wouldn't they all be one and the same?

The Jain philosophical school claims that mental defilements invade the nature of the mind and that for as long as the continuum of the mind lasts, the impressions will remain. Buddhists reply to this by saying that the very nature of the mind contains no flaws; disturbances concern adventitious circumstantial defilements which may be, among other things, afflicting emotions. I do not see why the actual continuum of the mind should have an end since it has no beginning. Once Buddhahood has been realized, a person's individual continuum continues to exist; we can speak in this case of the individual identity of a Buddha.

The Scriptures emphasize, however, the fact that all Buddhas have "the same taste" in the realm of emptiness. This is to be understood in terms of equality with regard to the qualities of their mind, their wisdom, etc. All Buddhas are equal and equivalent in the space of emptiness. According to the perspective of the Buddhas, all have the same abilities to help other sentient beings. But in the example of the two historic Buddhas, Kashyapa and Shakyamuni, according to the perspective of ordinary human beings, as we all have different karmas, we have closer karmic links with Guru Shakyamuni than with Buddha Kashyapa, who lived in a much more remote era.

Is auditory consciousness attentive to the silence between the perception of two sounds?

Possibly, because we can perceive the absence of sound. But is it really an auditory faculty? Is it truly the auditory consciousness which perceives silence?

What is the difference between realizing emptiness and recognizing the nature of the mind?

Emptiness, as described in the Sutras and Tantras, is not exactly the same as the nature of the mind. In the tantric context, the nature of the mind seems to be quite different from the emptiness of the mind. Tibetan scholars were divided over these two divergent views. According to one, as far as the view of emptiness is concerned, both Sutras and Tantras speak of the same thing. This position derives from an appreciation of objective emptiness, the emptiness of an object. The second school of thought supports the existence of differences in the subjective experience of emptiness. And it is true that from the point of view of the subjective comprehension of emptiness, when we are dealing with the recognition of the nature of the mind, the higher Tantras differ greatly from the tradition of the Sutras.

Can it be said that the Buddha is in a permanent state of Buddhahood if everything changes all the time?

In general, the concept of Buddhahood refers to the Dharmakaya, the ultimate body of a Buddha. One of numerous other aspects is his physical manifestation, the Nirmanakaya. Buddhahood has permanent and impermanent aspects; it results from a commitment to a spiritual path, associated with a process of purification and perfection. What do you mean by "permanent?" Immortality sometimes qualifies Buddhahood. We also say it is permanent. Take the activities of a Buddha: they are unceasing and omnipresent. A Buddha acts spontaneously, without the slightest interruption or stopping. In this respect we can qualify Buddhahood as permanent. The inborn clear light of the mind, or *rigpa* consciousness, is sometimes called *lhundrup*, spontaneous clear light. This indication describes Buddhahood in terms of non-origin, non-beginning. Although defilements and disturbances may be impressed upon the mind, its essential nature always remains fundamentally pure. This implies that there is no ultimate difference between samsara and nirvana.

Guru Jigmed Tenpe Nyima says that Buddhahood, a state without beginning, is not produced and is not composed. That does not mean that it is not the product of causes and conditions, but that its continuum is immutable and not produced. Therefore, from this point of view, it is permanent and never interrupted, whether it is in one state or another.

You have said that the ultimate truth is beyond the intellect. If the intellect cannot apprehend it, what can? How can it be known?

First of all, let us clarify the meaning ascribed to "intellect." Shantideva has said in the *Bodhicharyavatara* that the ultimate truth is not an object of the intellect. Here, "ultimate truth" means emptiness, and "intellect" refers to dualistic consciousness. Certain passages of the *Madhyamakavatara,* the "Entrance to the Middle" by Chandrakirti, are similar to this assertion when they speak of the cessation of consciousness in Buddhahood. We must therefore distinguish between the intellect as gross consciousness and a much more subtle form. Intellect, *lo* in Tibetan, refers mainly to a certain type of consciousness. The proposition can take on a much broader meaning; when it is said that ultimate truth is not an object of the intellect, we should not imagine that ultimate truth cannot be apprehended by a form of intellect, but rather that dualistic consciousness—that of conceptual thought—cannot be. To be more precise, I would add that ultimate truth cannot be directly perceived by dualistic consciousness, by conceptual thought that operates only by means of images and concepts.

Here is another example which will help you understand what Shantideva is saying: Kunu Lama Rinpoche was in the habit of quoting the Nyingma Pandit Rong Zompa, who maintained that in Buddhahood there is neither consciousness, nor wisdom, nor transcendent knowledge. However, Longchenpa, another master of the Nyingmapa tradition, claimed the opposite. This school is therefore divided between two diverging views regarding the existence of consciousness and wisdom in Buddhahood. In one of his texts, Guru Jigmed Tenpe Nyima gives a quote by the Terton Kepo from a text of the Maha Yoga tradition, to the effect that the mind, *sem* in Tibetan, exists even in Buddhahood. Does the mind, from the point of view of its separation from primordial intelligence—rigpa in Tibetan—exist in enlightenment or not? This is the problem we now have to consider. On the other hand, the mind—as understood in the generally accepted use of the word as comprising all sorts of consciousnesses and intelligences—does certainly exist in Buddhahood. It is therefore important to be aware of the meaning of words depending on their context.

Let us take for example the term rigpa, in Sanskrit: *vidya*—it can have different meanings, sometimes that of consciousness in a general sense, a generic term covering all states of consciousness both manifest and non-manifest; at other times its meaning is much more precise and specific when it refers to original consciousness. Rigpa, in your question, is used in the sense of a penetrating view as opposed to an ignorant state of mind. As ignorance is, in certain respects, an aspect of consciousness, a certain way of knowing, we can easily affirm that it is a form of rigpa, bearing in mind the contrast which opposes the penetrating view of primordial intelligence to the ignorant mind.

What the Madhyamika texts have to say about the significance of language is so true! They affirm that the meaning of words does not evolve without control, that most often it is linked to the intention of the user, an intention which depends, among other things, on the context and the frame of reference. This is why rigpa will not necessarily mean the same thing, depending on the user and the context and the moment of its use. We mustn't place blinders on language!

Regarding your question, it is important to understand the meaning of the word "ultimate." In the *Uta Namche,* "Discernment of the Middle from the Extremes," Maitreya uses this term in three ways: the ultimate meaning refers to emptiness, the ultimate goal is nirvana, and the ultimate means are the Way. In another context, it will be understood in yet another way. Ultimate, in your question, refers to what must be denied. When we affirm that phenomena have no ultimate existence, we are thinking of their objective, independent status, as apprehended by ignorance. Ultimate can also be used in the context of how we should apprehend wisdom, that is, the penetrating view realizing emptiness. We sometimes consider the understanding of emptiness to be ultimate mind.

The idea of emptiness can give rise to a fear of being alone, a feeling of isolation. And indeed there is nothing—no object, no person to hold on to, no one to love. How can one eliminate this fear and go further into the understanding of emptiness?

I think you are confusing emptiness with a void, with nothingness. My advice is that you seek to understand emptiness from within the interdependence of phenomena. Usually we insist heavily upon the principle of interdependence in order to understand emptiness. Why not use the procedure in reverse? Because phenomena and events are devoid of inherent existence, we say that they are empty. As their existence is that of production determined by causes and conditions, we say that they are interdependent. Although the realization of emptiness from within interdependence is known to be very difficult, you will certainly manage to overcome your fear by paying particular attention to this aspect.

Take the case of deity yoga meditation; one of its aspects is the dissolution of all phenomena into emptiness, and it happens that at this stage of the practice we can feel isolation due to the total disappearance of all appearances into a state of voidness, a sort of nothingness. I wonder if the fear you speak of has not come about as a result of the visualizations of deity yoga, where all appearances are dissolved into this state of emptiness, or if this feeling of isolation stems from meditations on emptiness, the voidness of existence per se. It is extremely important to understand the distinction between the two, in order to be able to reach a clear identification of the primary origin of your fear. If this fear occurs during your meditations on emptiness, it might be one of two kinds: one is like a shock, as if you have been taken by surprise. This panic is totally natural and understandable; we might even say it is expected. Why? Because before this experience, all your conceptions of existence were solid, rigid; you perceived phenomena as if they had an independent, autonomous existence. A correct understanding of emptiness will eliminate your fear in an equally natural manner. And if this fails to happen, the second sort of fear would take over, given the fact that it is associated with an erroneous understanding comparable to nihilism, the feeling that nothing exists, that nothing matters.

How and why can we go on living day after day in a world that has no existence, since even the goal, Buddhahood, does not exist? Why should we seek to follow the path, and what is the meaning of life?

During my most recent trip to England, where I gave a series of lectures and teachings, someone asked me this question: "If phenomena and events have no existence or inherent identity, it is practically impossible to speak of identity as such. What must one do to establish it with certainty?" Upon hearing this I realized that this person had really given a great deal of thought to the problem, for it reflects the most sensitive point of Madhyamika philosophy. When this school of thought uses expressions such as "simple name" or "simple denomination," the word "simple" does not deny the reality of phenomena or their existence distinct from that name. It does not mean that there is nothing other than the name or the designation. To speak of a simple name, a simple imputation, or a simple designation is not to deny external objects. Since a phenomenon is an interdependent product, it must exist. To speak of the emptiness of a phenomenon is to envision its ultimate nature; it must therefore exist if we are to have knowledge of its ultimate reality. If, on the other hand, we seek the true referent hidden behind the term, the concept, we will find nothing. The object of the search cannot be found. Therefore, its existence can only be envisioned on a level of what is phenomenal, relative, and conventional, and not ultimate or absolute.

If we affirm that all phenomena are nothing but mental constructs, in the form of simple denominations, this does not imply that everything the mind can construct becomes reality, for if that were the case we would lapse into an extreme relativism far removed from the Madhyamika philosophy. Any extreme certifying that everything the mind can construct has an objective reality must be avoided. Nor should we conclude that the mind creates nothing. Between the phenomenon and the mind there is a certain relation, but as the product of the mind does not correspond to the true reality of the phenomenon, this generates illusions and false appearances. The mind, or rather, the consciousness which constructs such erroneous projections, becomes perverted in turn, for it does not agree with reality.

Let us take the example of the text here before me. Here in France you have an exquisite variety of bread known as baguette; if you look at this text from a distance and think it is a baguette, it makes no difference how insistent your belief in this is—you will not change the nature of the book into bread. You will never be able to change the book's reality. If you insist that you see only a baguette, this is an illustration of an imaginative process, a fiction created by the mind, without the slightest foundation in reality. The perception of the person who sees a book, however, is valid, because it corresponds to reality. There is a correspondence between the object in front of me and the perception a consciousness makes of it. We are dealing with two types of perception which, on their level, belong to the domain of appearances. One apprehends the appearance of a baguette, the other a book. One is altered and false, the other valid and truthful. But if we ask a third person to verify exactly what the object on the table is, he might remove all doubt and eliminate misunderstanding, invalidating the perception of bread in order to confirm the perception of the book, by going up to the table, touching the object, and saying: "This is not bread, this is a book." This perception cannot be invalidated, it remains valid in the context of conventional truth: the mind perceives the presence of a book which exists, there, on the table. Such a perception is not the fruit of an ultimate philosophical way of thinking, and that is why we cannot invalidate its relative reality through ultimate analysis. The perception of bread, however, can be easily rejected and invalidated by the correct perception of the book.

Here is another example: the Chittamatra philosophical school, known as the "Mind Only" school, posits the fundamental existence of a storehouse consciousness at the base of all our experiences. An ultimate analysis of this consciousness can invalidate this assertion, because it is not of a conventional nature. It is an ultimate philosophical point of view which can be rejected by a philosophical examination analyzing the ultimate nature of that reality.

To get back to the book on the table, its existence can be verified by a conventionally valid subjective criterion, a perception which cannot be invalidated by either another valid conventional experience or an ultimate analysis. But if we want to know exactly what this book is—if it is the sum of its pages, if each page is also the book, and so on—we will eventually come to the conclusion that the very concept of the book disappears. By breaking the book up into parts, pages, forms, colors, and so on, right down to its most elementary constituents—atoms and particles, etc.—the very idea of a solid text no longer exists. We will have reached a point which, to coin a phrase, might be called the "unfindableness" of the text as we know it. But what is certain is that the text does exist. We cannot deny its reality, although the ultimate analysis of what constitutes the true referent hidden behind the word "text" comes up with nothing, given the total impossibility of localizing it. The conclusion to be drawn from these comments is that as the text does exist, even if it proves unfindable as soon as we begin an ultimate search for it, its only possible mode of existence is nominal, conventional, and relative.

It is only possible to distinguish existence from existence per se on the level of experience, as with time our intellectual understanding of emptiness increases. The more we progress in this knowledge and its direct experience, the more the latter will discrimate between what is inherent existence and what is not. That is the heart of the problem. At the moment, phenomena may seem to us to be solid and concrete, as if they had a form of objective reality; this is in direct contradiction with another reality, the absence of independent existence. The more we perfect our understanding of emptiness, the more we will be capable of refuting inherent existence; the consequences of this negation will lead to what we call simple conditioning, where at this degree of understanding, the simple appearance of an object causes us to realize the emptiness of its nature, and the realization of this emptiness brings with it the even greater conviction of the apparent existence of the object.

I think it must be possible to determine this level of reality solely through experience, after we have satisfactorily rejected the inherent and independent existence of phenomena. As I have not attained this accomplishment, it is difficult for me to talk about it. No methods other than reflection and meditation on emptiness lead to this realization, to this level of reality which is reality. It is in this way that reality must be understood: on the level of the simple name, the simple designation, and an absence of inherent, independent, and autonomous existence. This is what has been accepted by the Buddhist philosophy of the Middle Way.

To sum up, when we distinguish between self and others, between samsara and nirvana, between all the polarities we have established, we perceive them as if they had a sort of objective, independent existence, which might be described as the true referent of each of these terms—"self," "others," "samsara," "nirvana," etc. This duality of polarities proves that we attribute to phenomena an independent and inherent existence, an existence in itself which is the very object to be rejected during our meditations on emptiness.

You have said that the human mind cannot examine itself, just as a sword cannot cut itself. Yet experience has shown that the mind can just as easily examine an external object as it can apprehend itself. The mind can seek to know itself, to know its qualities and its nature. For example, our mind observes that it is immaterial, that it is endowed with consciousnesses, that its purpose is to seek to understand and to know, just as the eye seeks to look and the hand seeks to touch. The analogy between the mind and the sword is not valid because the sword is a conceptual object which has no function in relation to itself. The hand, however, can touch itself and thus apprehend its own form. What do you think of this?

We can, of course, meditate on mental calm by using the mind as the object of concentration. It is also the mind which perceives its own nature. But we are dealing with different types of mind. The self-cognitive faculty of the mind is another thing, however, a distinct category of consciousness which is examined by schools of philosophy. When Yeshe Nyingpo, in his commentary on the ninth chapter of the *Bodhicharyavatara*, rejects the concept of *svasamvedana,* the self-cognitive faculty, the necessary distinction becomes quite clear. Partisans of the svasamvedana divide the mind into two basic main categories; one focuses on external objects, and the other has the faculty of self-knowledge and is said to be apperceptive and nondualistic, unable to perceive any external reality whatsoever. Shantideva's text denies this faculty but does not exclude the mind's capability of perceiving another mind or its own nature. According to the preceding views, if you accept the apperceptive faculty of the mind, after careful observation you will find that it is a particular type of mind which knows itself. This is why we cannot prove in a coherent way that such a mind has a function.

Is the mind an intrinsic part of the body? Does it need a body to exist? Is it the expression of a more vast and universal body, similar to the third body of a Buddha, the Dharmakaya?

I believe we must first distinguish between the gross and subtle levels of the body. The very subtle body can never be separated from the mind. Like the mind, it is without beginning or end. It is this body which will attain Buddhahood. Gross consciousnesses are associated with the gross levels of the human body, for example, and their existence will cease at the death of the body; that is to say that the human mind will cease to exist along with the human body with which it is associated. They are mutually dependent. However, human consciousnesses can exist only according to a support of the same nature; this support is the fundamental clear light of the mind. This very subtle mind does not depend on the physiological conditions of the body in order to exist. This is why it is possible to imagine a state where the subtle mind can exist separately from the gross body of our human existence. This subtle consciousness does, however, have an inseparable part, and that is subtle energy, which is in itself a form of the subtle body.

You have said that an individual must use up the aggregates which make up the body and mind in order to eliminate suffering. Does this mean that one must also dissolve our human form and that of others?

From the point of view of the individual, the purification of the aggregates results in the cessation of samsaric existence. But from a general point of view, samsara has no end. The sixteen classifications of emptiness indicate that the emptiness of samsara has neither beginning nor end. In this respect we need not worry about whether the world is presumed to come to an end or not. Every being possesses Buddhanature, the clear light of the mind. The question is whether, given this potential, we will be able to realize full enlightenment. We all have this potential, but as sentient beings are infinite in number, innumerable, we cannot really conceptualize a definitive end to samsara in its entirety.

You have said that the innate nature of the mind is luminous and pure. Why are we never able at any time in our life to spontaneously perceive it?

But we can nevertheless experience it, right? According to the explanations of the New School of Translation, it has been said that the nature of the mind, the subtle clear light, does not appear and cannot operate as long as the gross levels of the mind, such as sensory perceptions and conceptual thought processes, remain active. It remains present in a dormant form. In Dzogchen, there is a specific technique enabling one to recognize the rigpa, the primordial consciousness, without having to dissolve the gross states of the mind. Just as oil penetrates the entire sesame seed, the essential nature of clear light penetrates every experience of the mind. This is why the experience of recognition of this primordial consciousness—the essential nature of the mind which is clear light—is possible, even if sensory perceptions and mental processes have not completely ceased. But in any case, it can only be recognized by virtue of an inner experience. It is impossible to observe the nature of the mind with the eye, or to provide an explanation for it or a valid description in words.

Why can we not experience this nature spontaneously? Because it is very subtle. You know that emptiness is the ultimate nature of the mind, but it is only through analysis and experience that you will be able to perceive it. If we push the issue even further and ask why it is impossible to realize these subtle points spontaneously, I would answer that this is completely natural, in the order of things.

Isn't it against the law of evolution to be reborn after a human life in the body of an animal?

The theory of evolution must be understood in terms of physical evolution. To imply that a human being can become an animal in his next life has no connection with physical evolution but refers to a very different aspect, concerning consciousness and its capability to manifest in other forms of life.

If someone is reborn as a member of a lesser species, can they create enough positive karma to be reborn as a human being?

In general it is difficult, but given certain circumstances it would seem that the karmic potential accumulated during past lives may become active and result in a favorable rebirth. For this to happen we must, of course, have imprinted upon our flow of consciousness a positive karmic potential before having fallen into a lower realm of rebirth.

Does chance have a place in a Buddhist context, or is everything based exclusively on the law of the interdependence of phenomena and the notion of karma?

My overall response to this is to say that it depends on karma. Let us take our own personal everyday experience and consider the times where we say, quite easily, "Look, I'm lucky today!" or "What bad luck!" Although we use such expressions, I think we must relate our daily experiences to the concept of karma. So many different factors contribute to the causes and conditions of an act that we must take them into account and know how to make the distinction between a cause and its conditions. This is not an easy thing for us to do even on a superficial level. So many factors make up so-called circumstantial conditions. We might say that something happened by chance—blindly, as it were—for no apparent reason. That is the problem: the reasons are not at all clear.

As long as we remain in the context of the law of karma, I favor the following explanation: when events reach a point where we feel a pleasant or unpleasant sensation, that is the karma becoming apparent. If you deny the intervention of karma, you could establish, through the lineage of your parents, grandparents, and all your ancestors, that the continuum of your body ultimately returns to the origin of our universe. But the tantric system of Kalachakra describes the original substratum of the physical world of this present universe as a space of particles left over from the end of one universe before the creation of another. All matter is condensed into these particles, which are the physical factor contributing to all physical manifestations. The continuity of this process can in no way be ascribed to karma; it is a natural evolution. Although all the space particles are of the same nature, they have varied reactions among themselves, and in this way create animate objects like the human body, and other, inanimate objects, for example, rocks.

Let us not forget that the sentient being and the environment are interconnected. This relation is of a karmic nature. I do not think, however, that we can explain the continuity of the evolutionary process of the formation of the universe by karma. We cannot say that karma activates that process, nor attribute it to the power of the Buddhas. Moreover, what about the fact that all phenomena are devoid of inherent existence? This emptiness is not a product of karma, nor is the capacity of sentient beings to feel joy or sorrow a product of karma. The various capacities and potentialities of chemical components cannot be attributed to karmic influence, but rather to the laws of nature. At what stage does karma begin to play an active role, and up to what point are we dealing with the laws of nature alone? This is very interesting terrain for research, where we must seek to understand where natural laws leave off and where the evolving influence of karma begins. Look at this tulip here, in front of me: the fact that it is here is, I think, without doubt connected to a karmic influence. But karma has nothing to do with the amount of water or sunlight it needs in order to grow; these are considerations belonging to the chemical composition of the flower, which have nothing to do with karma.

We can therefore interpret luck or chance on different levels.

You gave the example of the flower, saying that its chemical reactions were not linked to karma, but that the presence of the tulip could be a result of karma. Could you go into more detail?

A flower may grow as a result of chemical reactions; this is natural law. Why do effects result from causes? What is the relation between cause and effect? This is a natural principle in which karma plays no role. It is just the law of causality. The principle of karma can only operate within the principle of causality of which it is, in a way, only a part. The law of causality covers much more ground than the principle of karma operating within it. We cannot attribute the law of causality entirely to the principle of karma.

Let us take a tree which has thousands of leaves of varying shades of yellow. In autumn they take on different reddish shades. What makes some leaves more yellow than others? Why do some become more reddish? Just as when the leaves fall, some blow far away, others pile up near the tree trunk; in any case, they do not all drop from the tree at the same time. I cannot see how karma could have any specific activity conditioning this natural process. How could karma make some leaves scatter to the east, others to the south? But the tiny microscopic animals who live on the leaves and fall with them are subject to the principle of karma; I think karma plays a part in the fact that they are losing their shelter, for example. I do not however have any definitive opinions on this topic. Whatever the case, it is clear that the law of causality is a natural principle produced neither by a Buddha nor by prayers, or even karma. It is simply natural law.

All other laws, such as those of karmic process, can operate on this basis. An interaction between the causes and effects of karma can occur if the natural law of causality is the basis of that interaction; thus, certain events can lead to other events which, in turn, will produce others, and so on. The interaction of diverse substances can also give rise to other processes, varied potentialities. A clear understanding of the ins and outs of the different laws governing the world of phenomena will enable us to see that a given cause produces a given effect, that *this* leads to *that*. It is impossible to explain the principle of karma without accepting that there is a law of nature underlying the other principles. When someone asks me why virtuous acts result in beneficial effects and negative acts lead to unpleasant consequences, I can only answer: "That's the way it is; it's natural." There is no logical explanation.